COOK it
Your Way

WeightWatchers®

COOKit Your Way

TAMSIN BURNETT-HALL

Over **95 RECIPES** to help you *eat* WHAT you like WHEN you like

**SIMON &
SCHUSTER**

London · New York · Sydney · Toronto · New Delhi

A CBS COMPANY

the recipes

 ProPoints values: You'll find a **ProPoints** value beside every recipe in this book. This tells you how many **ProPoints** values per serving each recipe contains.

Filling & Healthy Foods: We highlight all of our Filling & Healthy foods in green. These foods are at the heart of our plan so eat them where you can – they will help to fill you up faster and keep you fuller for longer.

 This means you can freeze this dish. There may be specific freezing instructions so just check the recipe to be sure.

the small print

EGGS We use medium eggs, unless otherwise stated. Pregnant women, the elderly and children should avoid recipes with eggs which are not fully cooked or raw.

FRUIT AND VEGETABLES Our recipes use medium-sized fruit and veg unless otherwise stated.

LOW FAT SPREAD When a recipe uses a low fat spread, we mean a spread with a fat content of no less than 38%.

LOW FAT SOFT CHEESE Where a recipe uses low fat soft cheese, we mean a soft cheese with a fat content of less than 5%.

MICROWAVES If we have used a microwave in any of our recipes, the timings will be for an 850 watt microwave oven.

PREP AND COOKING TIMES These are approximate and meant to be guidelines. Prep time includes all the steps up to and following the main cooking time(s). Cooking times may vary according to your oven. Before serving chicken, always check that there is no pink meat and that the juices run clear by piercing with a sharp knife or skewer.

The use of the words 'gluten free' or the 'gluten free icon' is purely informative. Weight Watchers is not responsible for the potential existence of gluten in dishes that have not been prepared in accordance to instructions or any other external cause. Recipes that are labelled as gluten free or that display this icon only contain ingredients in their natural state that do not originally contain gluten. However, in case of processed or canned foods consumption – or foods elaborated in any other way to prepare the dishes – it is essential to ensure that the ingredient in question does not include gluten itself. The user should refer to the information available on the product label and, if in doubt, contact the manufacturer or supplier of the relevant ingredient.

First published in Great Britain by Simon & Schuster UK Ltd, 2015
A CBS Company

Copyright © 2015, Weight Watchers International, Inc.

Simon & Schuster UK Ltd
222 Gray's Inn Road
London WC1X 8HB
www.simonandschuster.co.uk
Simon & Schuster Australia, Sydney
Simon & Schuster India, New Delhi

This book is copyright under the Berne Convention.
No reproduction without permission.
All rights reserved.

10 9 8 7 6 5 4 3 2 1

Weight Watchers, **ProPoints** and the **ProPoints** icon are the registered trademarks of Weight Watchers International Inc. and used under license by Weight Watchers (UK) Ltd.
All rights reserved.

Weight Watchers Publications Team:
Imogen Prescott, Nicola Kirk, Stephanie Teed
Photography: William Shaw
Food preparation: Penny Stephens
Prop styling: Liz Hippisley
Hand models: Scarlet Adam, Stephanie Teed, Nicola Kirk, Penny Stephens

For Simon & Schuster
Senior Commissioning Editor: Nicky Hill
Art Director: Corinna Farrow
Production Manager: Katherine Thornton
Design: Miranda Harvey

Colour Reproduction by Aylesbury Studios Ltd, UK
Printed and bound in Germany

A CIP catalogue record for this book is available from the British Library

ISBN: 978-1-47114-206-2

Pictured on front cover, clockwise from top left: Banana & berry drop scones, page 24; Cajun sirloin steak, page 150; Mocha walnut brownies, page 192; Super-quick lamb baguette with onions, page 154

Contents

Weight Watchers & the *ProPoints* PLAN

Weight Watchers gives you all the tools to help you achieve your weight loss goals and will enable you to adapt the plan according to your personal preferences.

ProPoints values

Keep an eye out for the **ProPoints** bucket. Inside will be a number which tells you the amount of **ProPoints** values each serving is and therefore how many you'll need to use from your daily allowance. This makes it really easy to follow the plan while cooking from scratch as there is no guesswork involved.

Personalising the plan

Gluten free, high protein, Mediterranean style. Over the last few years eating habits have changed. In a big way. So we've gathered together the most popular and created a range of effective approaches that allow you to eat the way you like with Weight Watchers. Say you don't do gluten, we'll offer you an approach that doesn't include gluten. And if protein's your thing, we'll suggest an approach that's higher in protein and lower in carbs. That's because we're fully flexible and can offer the support and expertise to help you eat what you like, the way you like, and still lose weight.

How this cookbook can work best for you

If you like the sound of all this flexibility then simply look for the icon that appeals to you. If you're after a low carb recipe then look at the table on pages 8–11 and you'll see at a glance which recipes are Lower Carb and the icon to look out for. So no matter which approach you've decided to follow, this cookbook will be the perfect companion.

Find out more at www.weightwatchers.co.uk

Filling & Healthy day approach

A great way to get focused on your weight loss. And an alternative way to follow the plan if you don't want to weigh, measure and count everything. The Filling & Healthy day approach introduces you to an alternative to counting the **ProPoints** values of everything you eat and drink. You simply focus your eating on our list of hundreds of Filling & Healthy foods. These foods help to fill you up faster, stay fuller for longer and avoid the types of foods that can lead to overeating. We've included loads of recipes in this book that are perfect for when you're following this approach – just look out for the little green heart beside the recipe and job's done!

Gluten Free approach

This approach will steer you to food choices that are naturally gluten free. The **ProPoints** plan is flexible enough to accommodate all your gluten free choices. To make it easy we've flagged the recipes in this book that are suitable for the Gluten Free approach; but with some of the ingredients used please do make sure you check the product labels (we've pointed out where) – sometimes a cheeky little stock cube, soy sauce or even ketchup can contain gluten.

Higher Carb approach

Passionate about pasta? Can't live without daily bread? Here's how to have your cake and eat it. If you love your carbs, we'll help you make smarter choices for healthy weight loss. There's no need to deny yourself, whether you're on a Filling & Healthy day or counting your daily allowance. Fill your plate with wholewheat pasta and know you're on safe ground with baked spuds. Opt for wholewheat and wholegrain every time: it's easy to embrace your complex carbs. We've made it easy for you to find the Higher Carb recipes in this book by using the HC icon. Check out the delicious Chilli Crab Spaghetti on page 160 for a carb-tastic dinner.

Mediterranean approach

Serve up sunshine on a plate. For fresh, delicious food, simply served and bursting with flavour, take a Mediterranean approach to your meals and snacks. This is a great approach if you love fish. Focus on our delicious meal ideas, serving up at least two fish dishes in your week with salads or a large bowl of veg. Opt for desserts and snacks of fresh fruit and natural yogurt and use healthier olive oil instead of butter. Flick to page 42 for a Med-inspired lunch fit for a Greek god.

Lower Carb approach

Try our lower carb, higher protein recipes for a lighter way to healthy weight loss. We're talking lower carbs here, not no carbs, as it's important to include some carbs in your eating every day. This approach is about lighter carbs and more of a focus on satisfying proteins. Go for lean cuts of meat such as fillet steak and skinless chicken breasts, or opt for Quorn, and combine with large servings of vegetables or salad. We've included some pretty tasty Lower Carb recipes in this book – you only need to look out for the LC icon to see what we mean.

Vegetarian approach

Whether you're a lifelong vegetarian or a part-timer – it can taste good to go meat-free. We've got loads of vegetarian recipes in this book; and if it's not got a little V icon bedside the recipe, check out the Cook's tips and Variations at the bottom of the recipe – it may be that we've given you an idea for swapping out the meat, meaning you can try out even more of the recipes in the book.

Note: Where relevant, free-range eggs, vegetarian cheese, vegetarian virtually fat-free fromage frais, vegetarian low fat crème fraîche and vegetarian low fat yogurts are used. Virtually fat-free fromage frais, low fat crème fraîche and low fat yogurts may contain traces of gelatine so they are not always suitable for a vegetarian diet – just check the labels.

Quick guide to Eating it Your Way

Recipe	♥	GF	HC	M	LC	V
SUPER STARTS						
Blueberry & pomegranate smoothie						Y
Mango blitz	Y	Y				Y
Must-try muesli			Y			Y
Banana & berry drop scones			Y			Y
Scrumptious apple & raisin pancake			Y			Y
Mango muesli muffins			Y			Y
Courgette fritters with smoked salmon				Y		
Spicy chorizo scrambled eggs					Y	
Ham & egg thins	Y				Y	
Really tasty egg-topped potatoes	Y	Y	Y	Y		Y
ON THE GO						
Vietnamese style prawn noddle wraps			Y			
Crunchy Mediterranean pittas			Y	Y		Y
Cheese & apple toasties			Y			Y
Curried potato & spinach frittata	Y	Y				Y
Little bacon & egg pies					Y	
Pastrami roll-ups with orzo pasta salad			Y			
Seared tuna & egg salad		Y		Y	Y	
Ham hock, Puy lentil & beetroot salad		Y	Y			
Warm chicken, avocado & bacon salad		Y			Y	
Tomato tuna & couscous salad			Y	Y		
Healthy Italian bean soup		Y	Y	Y		
Spiced carrot & lentil soup	Y	Y	Y			Y
Chunky chickpea soup & chorizo soup			Y			
OCCASIONS						
Posh seafood lasagne				Y	Y	
Sticky gingered salmon		Y		Y	Y	
Roast turkey & stuffing with special cranberry gravy						
Bacon topped chicken with mustard & mozzarella		Y			Y	
Sicilian meatball & orzo bake			Y			
Sausage & mash with a twist			Y			

Recipe	♥	GF	HC	M	LC	V
Steaks topped with creamy mushroom gratin		Y			Y	
Sunday best beef with honey roasted parsnips					Y	
Smoked paprika beef stew	Y	Y			Y	
Gorgeous pesto lamb		Y			Y	
Stilton & leek tartlets					Y	Y
Mexican tamale pie			Y			Y
Vegetarian stroganoff	Y		Y			Y

FAKEAWAYS

Recipe	♥	GF	HC	M	LC	V
Stir-fried chicken in oyster sauce			Y			
Crispy chicken with fries & coleslaw			Y			
Tandoori chicken with green chutney	Y	Y	Y			
Caesar turkey burgers						
Tex-Mex turkey			Y		Y	
Chinese duck wraps			Y			
Beef keema dhansak & fresh mango chutney	Y	Y			Y	
Massaman beef curry			Y		Y	
Lamb shawarma stuffed pittas						
Sesame prawns with sweet & sour noodles						
Keralan coconut fish curry		Y				
Fish fingers, chips & pea purée	Y		Y			
Ham & mushroom panzerotti			Y			
Quick pineapple stir-fried pork		Y			Y	
Mushroom fried rice with omelette strips	Y	Y	Y			Y
Creamy Thai vegetable curry		Y				Y

HOME AT 7 DINNER BY 8

Recipe	♥	GF	HC	M	LC	V
The nicest smoky chicken			Y	Y	Y	
Super-speedy tortilla pizza			Y			
One-pot chicken pilau	Y	Y	Y			
Southeast Asian chicken with cauliflower 'rice'	Y	Y			Y	
Sticky mango chicken with a lemon potato salad		Y	Y	Y		
One-dish Italian sausage			Y	Y		
Thai pork mince	Y	Y			Y	
Pan-fried pork & apples		Y	Y			
Must-try pasta spanakopita			Y	Y		Y
Quorn sausage pasta bake			Y			Y

Recipe	♥	GF	HC	M	LC	V
Cajun sirloin steak	Y	Y				
Hoisin beef & noodles			Y			
Super-quick lamb baguette with onions			Y			
Gorgeous lamb tagine			Y			
Cheesy smoked haddock & broccoli pots		Y			Y	
Chilli crab spaghetti			Y			
Mediterranean-inspired sea bass, potato & fennel		Y	Y	Y		

MAKE THE MOST OF 5

Recipe	♥	GF	HC	M	LC	V
Quick pea 'guacamole'	Y	Y				Y
Thai butternut squash soup		Y				Y
Best-ever root vegetable crisps		Y	Y	Y		Y
Home-made popcorn		Y	Y			Y
Turkey stir-fry with a kick	Y	Y			Y	
The best chicken kebabs	Y	Y		Y	Y	
Simple beef stew					Y	
Classic seafood stew		Y		Y	Y	
Oriental fish parcels	Y	Y				
Seafood cod with chilli broccoli		Y		Y	Y	
Butternut squash & goat's cheese frittata		Y		Y	Y	Y
Broccoli & blue cheese gratin		Y			Y	Y

DESSERTS & BAKES

Recipe	♥	GF	HC	M	LC	V
Mocha walnut brownies			Y			Y
Lemon & lime crunch cake			Y			Y
Banana & pistachio cupcakes			Y			Y
Ginger oat cookies			Y			Y
Tropical meringue crush		Y				Y
White chocolate puds with raspberry sauce		Y				
Apple & ginger fool		Y				Y
Layered cheesecake sundaes						Y
Bubbly jellies	Y	Y				
Strawberry layered puds					Y	Y
Apricot & raspberry popovers						Y
Pineapple tatins			Y			Y
Swedish apple & almond bake						Y
Marbled chocolate risotto			Y	Y		Y

Quick ProPoints VALUES index

Bubbly jellies
208

Mango blitz
20

Quick pea 'guacamole'
166

Thai butternut squash soup
168

Blueberry & pomegranate smoothie **18**

Best-ever root vegetable crisps
170

Ginger oat cookies
198

Tropical meringue crush
200

Little bacon & egg pies
48

Hearty Italian bean soup
60

Creamy Thai vegetable curry
126

Home-made popcorn
172

Turkey stir-fry with a kick
174

Oriental fish parcels
182

Mocha walnut brownies
192

Lemon & lime crunch cake **194**

Apple & ginger fool **204**

Mango muesli muffins **28**

Chunky chickpea & chorizo soup **64**

Stilton & leek tartlets **88**

Beef keema dhansak & fresh mango chutney **108**

The best chicken kebabs **176**

Simple beef stew **178**

Seared cod with chilli broccoli **184**

Butternut squash & goat's cheese frittata **186**

Banana & pistachio cupcakes **196**

White chocolate puds with rasp-berry sauce **202**

Strawberry layered puds **210**

Apricot & raspberry popovers **212**

Must-try muesli **22**

Banana & berry drop scones **24**

Courgette fritters with smoked salmon **30**

Vietnamese style prawn noodle wraps **40**

Crunchy Mediterranean pittas **42**

Cheese and apple toasties **44**

Ham hock, Puy lentil & beetroot salad **54**

Warm chicken, avocado & bacon salad **56**

Spiced carrot & lentil soup **62**

Keralan coconut fish curry **116**

Thai pork mince **142**

Classic seafood stew **180**

Broccoli & blue cheese gratin **188**

Swedish apple & almond bake **216**

Scrumptious apple & raisin pancake **26**

Really tasty egg-topped potatoes **36**

Curried potato & spinach frittata **46**

Pastrami roll-ups with orzo pasta salad **50**

Seared tuna & egg salad **52**

Tomato tuna & couscous salad **58**

Sticky gingered salmon **70**

Bacon topped chicken with mustard & mozzarella **74**

Steaks topped with creamy mushroom gratin **80**

Smoked paprika beef stew **84**

Quick pineapple stir-fried pork **122**

Super-quick lamb baguette with onions **154**

Mediterranean-inspired sea bass, potato & fennel **162**

Layered cheesecake sundaes **206**

Pineapple tatins **214**

Marbled chocolate risotto **218**

Spicy chorizo scrambled eggs **32**

Ham & egg thins **34**

Posh seafood lasagne **68**

Gorgeous pesto lamb **86**

Tex-Mex turkey **104**

One-dish Italian sausage **140**

Cheesy smoked haddock & broccoli pots **158**

Sausage & mash with a twist **78**

Mexican tamale pie **90**

Vegetarian stroganoff **92**

Caesar turkey burgers **102**

Mushroom fried rice with omelette strips **124**

Super-speedy tortilla pizza **132**

Must-try pasta spanakopita **146**

Roast turkey & stuffing with cranberry gravy **72**

Sunday best beef with honey roasted parsnips **82**

9 ProPoints value

Stir-fried chicken
in oyster sauce
96

9 ProPoints value

Tandoori chicken
with green chutney
100

9 ProPoints value

Chinese
duck wraps
106

Ham & mushroom
panzerotti
120

9 ProPoints value

The nicest
smoky chicken
130

9 ProPoints value

Southeast Asian
chicken with cauli-
flower 'rice' **136**

9 ProPoints value

Cajun
sirloin steak
150

Hoisin beef
& noodles
152

10 ProPoints value

Sicilian meatball
& orzo bake
76

10 ProPoints value

Crispy chicken with
fries & coleslaw
98

10 ProPoints value

Massaman
beef curry
110

10 ProPoints value

Lamb shawarma
stuffed pittas
112

10 ProPoints value

Sesame prawns
with sweet & sour
noodles **114**

10 ProPoints value

Fish fingers, chips
& pea purée
118

10 ProPoints value

One-pot chicken
pilau
134

10 ProPoints value

Sticky mango
chicken with a lemon
potato salad **138**

10 ProPoints value

Pan-fried pork
& apples
144

10 ProPoints value

Quorn sausage
pasta bake
148

10 ProPoints value

Gorgeous
lamb tagine
156

10 ProPoints value

Chilli crab
spaghetti
160

Quick *ProPoints* VALUES index

SUPER Starts

Blueberry & Pomegranate Smoothie

This vibrantly coloured breakfast drink is a marvellous way to start the day.

 ProPoints values per serving
ProPoints values per recipe 5

V Serves 2
Takes 5–10 minutes

2 tablespoons porridge oats
200 ml no added sugar
    pomegranate juice
60 g blueberries **(fresh or frozen)**
50 g fat-free natural yogurt
4 ice cubes

If you have time, soak the oats in the pomegranate juice for 5 minutes to soften them and give a smoother texture. However, it's not essential to do this if you're in a hurry.

Add the blueberries, yogurt and ice cubes to the oats and juice in a liquidiser (or you can use a hand-held blender) and blitz until smooth.

Divide between 2 glasses to serve.

Variation

Try using cranberry juice and raspberries, instead of the pomegranate juice and blueberries, for a pink power-start juice.

GF If you want to make this a gluten free recipe, simply replace the porridge oats with gluten free porridge oats, which are now widely available in many supermarkets.

Cook's tip Try adding a sliced banana to the mixture before blending if you prefer a thicker drink.

Mango BLITZ

 1 *ProPoints* value per serving
ProPoints values per recipe 1

 Serves 2
Takes 10 minutes

 2 oranges

 1 large ripe mango, peeled and
    flesh chopped roughly
100 g 0% fat natural Greek yogurt
6 ice cubes
juice of ½ lime

A delightfully fresh-tasting smoothie.

Using a sharp knife, cut the skin and white pith away from the oranges and then roughly chop the flesh, discarding any pips.

Put the orange and mango flesh in a blender or food processor (or use a hand-held blender) and blitz to a smooth purée.

Add the Greek yogurt and ice cubes and blitz again to combine, adding the lime juice to taste.

Pour into 2 glasses to serve.

Cook's tip If fresh mangoes aren't seasonally available at a good price, you can use frozen diced mango instead; in which case you won't need to add any ice cubes.

Must-try *Muesli*

 5 *ProPoints* values per serving
ProPoints values per recipe 31

 Serves 6
Takes 5 minutes

- 15 g pumpkin seeds
- 15 g sunflower seeds
- 15 g desiccated coconut
- 40 g ready to eat dried apricots, chopped small
- 25 g currants
- 200 g porridge oats

It's a matter of minutes to throw a batch of this muesli together, ready for a quick breakfast. Serve with 150 ml skimmed milk for an extra 1 *ProPoints* value per serving, and some chopped fresh or canned natural fruit to boost your daily fruit intake.

Place the seeds and coconut in a small non-stick frying pan, and toast over a medium heat for about 2 minutes until the seeds start to pop and the coconut turns golden. Tip them out on to a plate to cool.

Combine the apricots, currants and porridge oats in a mixing bowl, and then stir in the cooled seeds and coconut.

Store in an airtight container.

Serve 50 g muesli per portion.

> *Cook's tip* Toasting the seeds and coconut really brings out their flavour. Use a dry non-stick pan – there's no need to add any calorie controlled cooking spray.

Banana & BERRY Drop Scones

 5 *ProPoints* values per serving
ProPoints values per recipe 21

Serves 4
Takes 20 minutes

* **Drop scones only**

 125 g self-raising flour
a pinch of salt

 2 teaspoons caster sugar
1 egg
150 ml skimmed milk
250 g blueberries
calorie controlled cooking spray
2 bananas, sliced
150 g strawberries, quartered
200 g fat-free natural fromage frais
4 teaspoons honey, to drizzle

Don't think of this as a breakfast just for weekends. If you make the drop scones when you have more time, you can then wrap and freeze them in batches of four. Simply microwave (or toast lightly) to serve with the fresh fruit and fromage frais, for a midweek breakfast that feels utterly indulgent.

Sift the flour into a mixing bowl with the salt and then stir in the sugar. Make a well in the middle and break in the egg. Gradually whisk in the egg and the milk until you have a thick, smooth batter. Stir in 100 g of the blueberries.

Spray a non-stick frying pan with the cooking spray. Drop in 4 spoonfuls of blueberry-studded batter and cook for about 1½ minutes each side over a medium heat.

Keep the cooked drop scones warm while you make 3 further batches, to give a total of 16 drop scones.

Meanwhile, combine the rest of the blueberries with the sliced bananas and strawberries.

Serve 4 drop scones per person, topped with the fruit, fromage frais and a drizzle of honey.

Scrumptious *Apple & Raisin* Pancake

ProPoints values per serving
ProPoints values per recipe 35

Serves 6
Preparation time 15 minutes
Cooking time 30–35 minutes

2 cooking apples, peeled, cored and
   sliced thinly
40 g raisins
50 g light brown sugar
½ teaspoon ground cinnamon
calorie controlled cooking spray
4 eggs, beaten
150 ml skimmed milk
25 g low fat spread, melted
100 g plain flour
a pinch of salt
½ teaspoon icing sugar
300 g 0% fat natural Greek yogurt

Inspired by a traditional Dutch recipe, this oven-baked pancake is an ideal choice for a relaxed weekend breakfast.

Preheat the oven to Gas Mark 4/180°C/fan oven 160°C.

Toss the sliced apples, raisins, sugar and cinnamon together in a mixing bowl, and tip into a 23 cm diameter round baking dish that has been sprayed with the cooking spray. Bake for 15 minutes on the centre shelf until the apples are starting to soften.

Take the dish out of the oven and increase the oven temperature to Gas Mark 7/220°C/fan oven 200°C.

Whisk together the eggs and milk and add the melted low fat spread. Sift in the flour and salt, and whisk until you have a smooth batter.

Pour the batter over the apples and bake at the higher temperature for 15–20 minutes until the oven pancake is golden brown and set.

Dust the pancake with the icing sugar, cut into wedges, then serve with the Greek yogurt.

MANGO
Muesli Muffins

 4 *ProPoints* values per muffin
ProPoints values per recipe 48

 Makes 12
Preparation time 15 minutes
Cooking time 20 minutes

 calorie controlled cooking spray
½ large mango, peeled and
    chopped small
grated zest and juice of ½ lime
250 g self-raising flour
1 teaspoon bicarbonate of soda
1 teaspoon ground mixed spice
a pinch of salt
75 g caster sugar
60 g muesli
1 egg, beaten
50 g low fat spread, melted
225 g low fat natural yogurt
3 tablespoons skimmed milk

Grab one of these fruity muffins for breakfast on the go.

Preheat the oven to Gas Mark 6/200°C/fan oven 180°C and spray a 12-hole non-stick muffin tray with the cooking spray.

Combine the chopped mango with the lime zest and juice in a small bowl, and set aside to infuse.

Sift the flour, bicarbonate of soda, mixed spice and salt into a mixing bowl. Stir in the sugar and 40 g of the muesli.

Mix together the egg, melted low fat spread, yogurt and skimmed milk, then stir into the dry ingredients, stirring just enough to combine them, without over-mixing, as this would make your muffins tough and rubbery.

Gently stir in the lime-infused mango, and then spoon the muffin mixture into the prepared muffin tray. Sprinkle the remaining muesli on top.

Bake for 15–20 minutes until the muffins have risen, are golden brown and springy to the touch.

Cool in the tray for 10 minutes before turning out to finish cooling on a wire rack. Store in an airtight container.

Cook's tip Muffins are at their best when freshly baked. If they are a day or so old, you can refresh them by warming for 15 seconds in a microwave, but for optimum freshness the best option is to freeze the muffins on the day of baking. To defrost and warm through, heat a muffin in the microwave for 45–60 seconds.

Courgette Fritters with Smoked Salmon

 5 *ProPoints* values per serving
ProPoints values per recipe 22

 Serves 4
Preparation time 10 minutes
Cooking time 15 minutes

300 g courgettes, grated coarsely
150 g carrots, peeled and grated coarsely
100 g plain flour
1 egg
100 ml skimmed milk
3 tablespoons snipped fresh chives
calorie controlled cooking spray
salt and freshly ground black pepper

To serve
4 tomatoes, sliced
175 g smoked salmon
4 tablespoons Weight Watchers crème fraîche, or similar

If you're looking to impress, serve up these easy fritters, topped with delicious smoked salmon, for breakfast.

Squeeze handfuls of the grated courgettes and carrots over a bowl to remove the excess moisture. They should be quite dry before adding them to the batter.

Sift the flour and a pinch of salt into a mixing bowl then whisk in the egg and milk to give a thick, smooth batter. Stir in the squeezed-out courgettes and carrots plus half of the chives, and season the mixture with pepper.

Heat a non-stick frying pan on the hob and spray with the cooking spray. Drop in 4 generous spoonfuls of the vegetable batter and spread each one to about 9 cm diameter. Cook over a medium heat for 3–4 minutes each side until golden brown and cooked through. Keep warm while you cook another 4 fritters.

Serve 2 fritters per person, topped with the sliced tomatoes, smoked salmon, crème fraîche and a scattering of the remaining chives.

 Variation

Vegetarians can replace the smoked salmon with either a fried egg, for 7 *ProPoints* values per serving, or ½ an avocado, sliced thinly, and a shake of Tabasco sauce, for 5 *ProPoints* values per serving.

Spicy *Chorizo* Scrambled Eggs

 7 ProPoints value

ProPoints values per serving
ProPoints values per recipe 29

 Serves 4
Takes 15 minutes

½ x 150 g packet diced chorizo
1 red pepper, chopped small
8 eggs
6 tablespoons skimmed milk
calorie controlled cooking spray
4 slices Weight Watchers malted
   Danish bread, or similar
40 g baby leaf spinach
salt and freshly ground black
   pepper

Topped with chorizo and peppers, this Spanish-style twist on scrambled eggs makes a great brunch dish.

Fry the chorizo in a non-stick frying pan for 2 minutes until it starts to release its oil. Add the chopped pepper and cook for 3 minutes until softened.

Meanwhile, beat the eggs and milk with some seasoning. Spray a non-stick saucepan with the cooking spray and scramble the eggs over a low-medium heat, until cooked to your liking. Remember that the eggs will carry on cooking from the heat of the pan even when you take it off the hob, so make sure that you don't overcook them.

Toast the bread and top each slice with a handful of baby leaf spinach.

Spoon the scrambled eggs over the spinach and then top with the chorizo-pepper mixture. Serve immediately.

 Variation

Vegetarians can replace the chorizo with 150 g chopped mushrooms, which will reduce this dish to 6 *ProPoints* values per serving. Add 1 clove crushed garlic and a pinch of smoked paprika to give a fantastic smoky flavour boost.

> *Cook's tip* Chorizo is not a low fat ingredient, but it has such a robust flavour that you only need a small amount to deliver on the palate.

Ham & Egg Thins

 7 ProPoints value

 ProPoints values per serving
ProPoints values per recipe 13

 Serves 2
Takes 10 minutes

 LC

2 wholemeal sandwich thins, **split**
2 eggs
60 g quark
4 tomatoes, **sliced**
a few fresh basil leaves
100 g wafer thin ham
freshly ground black pepper

These easy but utterly tempting brunch thins make for an ideal lazy weekend breakfast, and are perfect if you're on a Filling & Healthy day.

Put the kettle on to boil and the sandwich thins on to toast.

Fill a small frying pan (or a saucepan) with boiling water. Add the whole eggs in their shells for just 20 seconds, then lift out with a draining spoon.

Crack the eggs into the water and cook at a very gentle simmer for 2–3 minutes, or until cooked to your liking.

Meanwhile, spread the toasted sandwich thins with quark and top with the tomatoes, basil and ham.

Lift the eggs out of their poaching water with a draining spoon and rest the spoon briefly on a wad of kitchen paper to absorb the excess liquid. Settle on top of the thins, season with pepper and serve.

Variation

If you prefer, you can fry the eggs in calorie controlled cooking spray in a non-stick frying pan.

Cook's tips For the best poached eggs, make sure that your eggs are as fresh as possible, as the whites are thicker and hold their shape around the yolk more easily. The same applies to fried eggs; so if you've ever wondered why sometimes they are nice and neat, and at others the white spreads out all over the pan, it is down to the freshness of the egg, because the white gets thinner over time.

Adding the whole eggs to boiling water for a few seconds helps to set their shape for poaching, so when you then break them into the poaching water you should end up with lovely tidy, picture-perfect poached eggs!

Really Tasty Egg-Topped POTATOES

6 *ProPoints* values per serving
ProPoints values per recipe 25

Serves 4
Preparation time 15 minutes
Cooking time 25 minutes

800 g potatoes, peeled and cubed
1 teaspoon smoked paprika
1 teaspoon ground coriander
1 teaspoon cumin seeds
1 red pepper, de-seeded and
   chopped
1 green pepper, de-seeded and
   chopped
250 g cherry tomatoes
calorie controlled cooking spray
2 tablespoons chopped fresh parsley
4 eggs
salt and freshly ground black
   pepper

These spiced sauté potatoes are cooked in the oven rather than on the hob, which is a far easier method! A runny-centred fried egg served on top of the potatoes makes for a delectable combination. Add a handful of raw baby spinach leaves, if you wish.

Preheat the oven to Gas Mark 7/220°C/fan oven 200°C and preheat a large baking tray on the top shelf.

Parboil the potatoes in boiling water for 5 minutes, covered.

Drain the potatoes, shake the spices into the pan with some seasoning and mix gently to coat. Combine with the peppers and tomatoes.

Spray the hot tray with the cooking spray and tip the spiced potatoes, peppers and tomatoes out on the hot tray and spray again. Roast in the oven for 20–25 minutes, stirring halfway through. The potatoes should be crisp at the edges, and the peppers and tomatoes starting to caramelise.

When the potatoes are almost ready, fry the eggs to your liking in a non-stick frying pan sprayed with cooking spray.

Divide the potatoes between 4 warmed plates, scatter with the parsley and top each plate with a fried egg. Serve immediately.

ProPoints values to spare? Scatter 25 g crumbled light feta cheese over the potatoes before topping with the egg, for an extra 1 *ProPoints* value per serving.

ON the Go

VIETNAMESE Style *Prawn* Noodle Wraps

 5 *ProPoints* values per serving
ProPoints values per recipe 20

 Serves 4
Takes 15 minutes

45 g dried vermicelli rice noodles
2 tablespoons hoisin sauce
juice of 1 lime
1 carrot, grated
7 cm cucumber, cut into shreds
½ red chilli, chopped finely
4 Weight Watchers tortillas, or
    similar
150 g cooked peeled king prawns
a few fresh coriander sprigs
salt and freshly ground black
    pepper

If you're bored with eating sandwiches at lunchtime, a filled wrap makes a good alternative. Inspired by Vietnamese summer rolls, juicy king prawns and aromatic vegetable noodles lend these tortilla wraps a Far Eastern twist.

Place the rice noodles in a bowl, cover with boiling water and leave to stand for 3–4 minutes until tender, or follow the packet instructions.

Mix the hoisin sauce with half of the lime juice and set aside.

Drain the noodles and combine with the rest of the lime juice, the carrot, cucumber and chilli, and season.

Warm the tortillas following the packet instructions, so that they are flexible and easy to wrap.

Divide the noodles between the tortillas, placing them across the centre of each one, then drizzle with the hoisin sauce mixture. Add the prawns and a few coriander sprigs, then roll up the wraps. Cut in half to serve.

Variation

Replace the king prawns with 150 g cooked skinless, boneless chicken breast, torn into shreds. The **ProPoints** values per serving will be 6.

Crunchy Mediterranean Pittas

ProPoints values per serving **5**
ProPoints values per recipe 22

Serves 4
Takes 10 minutes

10 g pumpkin seeds
3 ripe tomatoes, chopped roughly
5 cm cucumber, cubed
1 red pepper, cubed
8 olives in brine, sliced
40 g light feta cheese, crumbled
1 Little Gem lettuce, shredded
1 teaspoon extra virgin olive oil
2 tablespoons reduced fat houmous
2 tablespoons 0% fat natural Greek yogurt
4 Weight Watchers wholemeal pittas, or similar
salt and freshly ground black pepper

Toasted pumpkin seeds add a delicious crunch to these salad-filled pittas.

Toast the pumpkin seeds in a non-stick frying pan for 1–2 minutes until they start to pop. Remove from the heat.

Combine the pumpkin seeds, tomatoes, cucumber, red pepper, olives, feta cheese and lettuce in a bowl with the olive oil and some salt and black pepper.

Mix together the houmous and Greek yogurt.

Warm the pittas and split open, then spread each one with the houmous mixture.

Spoon the salad inside the pittas and serve immediately.

Cheese & APPLE Toasties

5 *ProPoints* values per serving
ProPoints values per recipe 9

 HC
Serves 2
Takes 10 minutes

 V
2 wholemeal sandwich thins
2 teaspoons grainy mustard
50 g mature half-fat vegetarian
   Cheddar cheese, grated
½ apple, sliced thinly

A quick and easy toasted sandwich; delicious served alongside either a big salad or a bowlful of zero *ProPoints* values soup.

Preheat the grill.

Split the sandwich thins open and spread each one with a teaspoon of mustard.

Divide the cheese between the two thins and add the sliced apple.

Press the top halves on, then grill the filled thins for about 2 minutes each side, until they are toasted on the outside and the cheese is melting inside.

Cut in half on the diagonal and serve immediately.

Variations

You can replace the apple with a sliced tomato or a little sliced onion, if you prefer. The ***ProPoints*** values per serving will be the same.

If you prefer, you can use 4 slices Weight Watchers thick sliced wholemeal bread, or similar, instead of the sandwich thins. The ***ProPoints*** values per sandwich will be 6.

Curried *Potato* & Spinach Frittata

 ProPoints values per serving
ProPoints values per recipe 24

 Serves 4
Takes 30 minutes

 500 g potatoes, peeled and cubed
½ teaspoon ground turmeric
calorie controlled cooking spray
a bunch of spring onions, sliced
1 teaspoon cumin seeds
½ teaspoon mustard seeds
1 teaspoon garam masala
100 g young leaf spinach
6 eggs, beaten
salt and freshly ground black
    pepper

A wedge of frittata makes a great lunch served with salad, and it tastes just as good served cold as when it's warm, making it perfect for a packed lunch or even for a picnic.

Add the potatoes and turmeric to a pan of boiling water. Cook for 10 minutes until tender, then drain.

Meanwhile, spray a non-stick frying pan (with a base measurement of 23 cm) with the cooking spray and fry the spring onions for 2–3 minutes.

Add the spices and potatoes to the frying pan and cook for 1–2 minutes, stirring until coated in the spices.

Mix the spinach into the potatoes until slightly wilted. Preheat the grill.

Beat the eggs, season, and pour over the potatoes and spinach, shaking the pan to level the contents. Cook over a low to medium heat for 7–8 minutes until the egg is mostly set.

Pop the pan under the grill (protecting the pan handle from the heat) and cook for 2–3 minutes until the top is set and golden. Leave to rest for 5 minutes in the pan before serving, cut into wedges.

Little *Bacon* & EGG Pies

 ProPoints values per serving
ProPoints values per recipe 21

 Makes 6
Preparation time 15 minutes
Cooking time 20 minutes

calorie controlled cooking spray
6 bacon medallions, snipped
a bunch of spring onions, sliced
3 x 45 g sheets filo pastry measuring
    50 x 24 cm, defrosted if frozen
2 eggs, beaten
100 ml skimmed milk
4 tablespoons Weight Watchers
    crème fraîche, or similar
salt and freshly ground black
    pepper

These tempting individual filo-crust pies can be served warm or cold, accompanied by a large mixed salad.

Preheat the oven to Gas Mark 4/180°C/fan oven 160°C.

Spray a non-stick frying pan with the cooking spray and cook the snipped bacon and spring onions for 5–6 minutes over a high heat until browned. Tip out on to a plate to cool.

Meanwhile, prepare the filo pie cases. Spray 6 holes of a 12-hole muffin tin with the cooking spray (use alternate holes to allow for the pastry rims to overlap the tin) and place the tin on a baking tray.

Cut the filo sheets in half and stack up as 6 squares. Working with one square at a time, spray with the cooking spray then fold it into quarters. Press this smaller layered square of filo into the prepared muffin tin, with the points overhanging the edges. Repeat with the remaining filo squares to make a total of 6 pie cases and spray each one with extra cooking spray.

Divide the bacon and spring onion mixture between the pie cases. Beat the eggs with the milk and crème fraîche, and season. Pour the egg mixture over the bacon filling and bake on the centre shelf for 15–18 minutes, or until the filling is set and just starting to puff up.

Serve warm or cold.

 Variation

For a vegetarian version, use 200 g sliced mushrooms in place of the bacon. Add a pinch of dried thyme as the mushrooms cook, and stir 25 g grated vegetarian hard Italian cheese into the egg mixture. The ***ProPoints*** values per serving will be 3.

Pastrami Roll-ups with Orzo Pasta Salad

 6 ProPoints value

ProPoints values per serving
ProPoints values per recipe 12

 HC

Serves 2
Takes 15 minutes

60 g dried orzo pasta
100 g broccoli, cut into small florets
60 g pastrami
60 g low fat soft cheese
25 g wild rocket
125 g cherry tomatoes, quartered
75 g sweetcorn
1 tablespoon low fat salad dressing
salt and freshly ground black
    pepper

A colourful orzo pasta salad accompanies spicy pastrami and soft cheese roll-ups in this lunchbox with a difference.

Add the orzo to a pan of boiling water and cook according to the packet instructions, adding the broccoli florets for the last 3 minutes of the cooking time.

Meanwhile, lay the pastrami slices out on a chopping board and add a dollop of low fat soft cheese at one end of each slice. Add a few rocket leaves and roll the pastrami up around the filling. Set aside.

Drain the orzo and broccoli and refresh in cold water. Tip back into the pan and stir in the cherry tomatoes, sweetcorn and salad dressing. Season to taste.

Divide the orzo pasta salad between 2 lidded containers, or bowls, place the remaining rocket on top and add the pastrami roll-ups.

 Variation

Vegetarians can replace the pastrami with Quorn Deli Style Peppered Beef Slices. The **ProPoints** values per serving will be 6.

> *Cook's tip* Orzo is a rice-shaped pasta that can be added to soups, served as a main meal accompaniment in place of couscous or, as here, used to form the basis of a salad.

Seared *Tuna* & Egg Salad

6 **ProPoints** values per serving
ProPoints values per recipe 12

Serves 2
Takes 15 minutes

2 eggs
100 g cucumber, cubed
3 ripe tomatoes, chopped roughly
½ yellow pepper, cubed
2 spring onions, sliced
6 radishes, sliced thinly
1 tablespoon shredded fresh basil
2 teaspoons lemon juice
1 teaspoon extra virgin olive oil
¼ teaspoon Dijon mustard
2 x 100 g fresh tuna steaks
calorie controlled cooking spray
1 Little Gem lettuce, leaves
    separated
salt and freshly ground black
    pepper

This summery chopped salad, topped with hard-boiled eggs and seared tuna, makes a fabulous quick lunch.

Add the eggs to a small saucepan of boiling water and cook for 7 minutes.

Meanwhile, combine the cucumber, tomatoes, pepper, spring onions, radishes and basil in a bowl.

Make a quick dressing by placing the lemon juice, olive oil, mustard, some salt and black pepper, and 1 teaspoon cold water in a jam jar and shake to mix (or whisk together in a small bowl). Pour the dressing over the chopped salad ingredients and stir to mix.

Preheat a griddle or non-stick frying pan. Season the tuna steaks and spray with the cooking spray. Griddle or pan-fry for about 2 minutes each side, or until cooked to your liking.

When the eggs are ready, drain and leave to cool in cold water for a couple of minutes. Shell the eggs and cut into quarters.

Divide the lettuce leaves between 2 plates or bowls and spoon the chopped salad on top. Add the quartered eggs and the tuna steaks and serve immediately.

Variation

For a transportable salad, replace the fresh tuna steaks with a 200 g can tuna steak in spring water, drained and flaked, and divided between the salads. The **ProPoints** values per serving will be 5.

Cook's tip Super-fresh eggs are not the best choice for hard-boiled eggs, as they are difficult to peel. Use eggs that are a few days old to make shelling much easier.

Ham Hock, Puy Lentil & BEETROOT Salad

 5 *ProPoints* values per serving
ProPoints values per recipe 11

 GF Serves 2
Takes 10 minutes

 HC

400 g can Puy lentils, rinsed and drained
100 g cooked natural beetroot, cubed
50 g raw sugar snap peas, sliced
1 tablespoon balsamic vinegar
3 tablespoons 0% fat natural Greek yogurt
½ teaspoon grainy mustard
75 g round lettuce leaves, separated
60 g shredded cooked ham hock
salt and freshly ground black pepper

Nutty Puy lentils combine beautifully with tasty beetroot, balsamic vinegar and crunchy sugar snap peas in this wonderfully substantial salad — perfect to chuck into a lunchbox and run!

Mix the lentils, beetroot and sugar snaps with the balsamic vinegar. Season and set aside.

In a small bowl, make a dressing by combining the yogurt and mustard. Season to taste.

Divide the lettuce between 2 bowls or lidded sandwich boxes. Spoon the lentils alongside and top with the shredded ham hock. Serve with a dollop of mustardy yogurt dressing.

Variations

If you prefer, the ham hock can be replaced by 2 x 35 g slices premium ham, chopped into matchsticks. The *ProPoints* values per serving will be 5.

V If you're a vegetarian, you'll love this served with 60 g light feta cheese crumbled over the lentil salad in place of the ham hock. The *ProPoints* values per serving will be 5.

Warm *Chicken*, AVOCADO & Bacon Salad

  5 *ProPoints* values per serving
ProPoints values per recipe 20

 GF

Serves 4
Takes 15 minutes

LC

350 g skinless chicken breast fillets
calorie controlled cooking spray
15 g pumpkin seeds
4 lean bacon medallions
150 g spinach, watercress and
rocket leaves
150 g cherry tomatoes, halved
½ avocado, sliced
4 tablespoons gluten free, low fat
salad dressing
salt and freshly ground black
pepper

If you want to take this salad to work rather than eat it warm, cook and cool the chicken and bacon in advance before adding to the salad ingredients.

Cut each chicken breast fillet in half horizontally to make two thin escalopes. Season and spray with the cooking spray. Cook on a preheated griddle or in a non-stick frying pan for 4–5 minutes, or until cooked through.

Meanwhile, toast the pumpkin seeds in a small frying pan for 2 minutes, or until starting to pop. Tip the seeds into a bowl then cook the bacon medallions for a couple of minutes each side. Remove to a plate and snip into pieces.

Divide the salad leaves, cherry tomatoes and avocado between 4 bowls. Drizzle with the dressing and sprinkle with the pumpkin seeds and bacon.

Slice the cooked chicken and place on top of the salad. Serve immediately.

 Variation

If you're vegetarian you could replace the chicken and bacon with 25 g crumbled goat's cheese per person. The ***ProPoints*** values per serving will be 5.

> ***Cook's tip*** To cut down on the preparation time, you can use 75 g ready-cooked skinless, boneless chicken breast per person, torn into chunky pieces, and ½ slice premium ham per person, chopped roughly, to replace the bacon. The *ProPoints* values per serving will be 5.

Tomato TUNA & Couscous Salad

Serves 1
Takes 5 minutes

40 g dried wholewheat couscous
5 tablespoons boiling water
¼ red, yellow or orange pepper,
   cubed
50 g cucumber, cubed
6 cherry tomatoes, quartered
15 g wild rocket
80g can Weight Watchers Tuna in
   Tomato & Herb Dressing
calorie controlled cooking spray
salt and freshly ground black
   pepper

This couscous salad is very quick and easy to assemble.
The tomato and herb sauce that coats the tuna dresses the
salad as you eat it, and packs a real flavour punch.

Place the wholewheat couscous in a small bowl and pour on the
boiling water. Season, stir, and cover with a plate. Leave to stand and
swell for 4–5 minutes while you prepare the salad vegetables.

When the couscous is ready, stir in the chopped pepper, cucumber
and cherry tomatoes. Tip the couscous salad into a lidded container if
you're planning to transport it, or transfer to a shallow bowl.

Top with the rocket leaves, and keep chilled. Add the tuna in tomato
and herb dressing when you're ready to eat.

Hearty ITALIAN
Bean Soup

 3 *ProPoints* values per serving
ProPoints values per recipe 10

 Serves 4
Preparation time 10 minutes
 Cooking time 25 minutes

 calorie controlled cooking spray
6 bacon medallions, snipped
1 onion, chopped
2 celery sticks, chopped
1 leek, chopped
3 carrots, chopped small
3 garlic cloves, crushed
½ teaspoon dried mixed herbs
500 g carton passata with basil
750 ml gluten free chicken stock
410 g can cannellini beans, rinsed
    and drained
80 g green cabbage, shredded
salt and freshly ground black
    pepper
fresh basil leaves, to garnish

A big bowl of this rustic soup, packed to the brim with vegetables, bacon and beans, will fill you up when you're running low on *ProPoints* values.

Spray a large, lidded, flameproof casserole with the cooking spray and add the bacon, onion, celery, leek, carrots and garlic. Season and cook, stirring occasionally, for 10 minutes.

Add the dried mixed herbs, the passata and stock. Bring to the boil and simmer, covered, for 10 minutes.

Stir in the cannellini beans and the cabbage and cook for 4–5 minutes.

Ladle into warmed bowls and serve garnished with fresh basil leaves.

 Variation

For a vegetarian variation, omit the bacon and replace the chicken stock with vegetable stock. The *ProPoints* values per serving will be 2.

Cook's tip Leeks often have grit trapped in between their layers. The best way to deal with this is to cut down through the top half of the leek and then fan out the layers under a running tap to rinse out any grit and dirt, then shake dry and slice the leeks.

SPICED *Carrot* & Lentil Soup

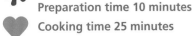 ProPoints values per serving
ProPoints values per recipe 31

* Serves 6
Preparation time 10 minutes

♥ Cooking time 25 minutes

calorie controlled cooking spray
1 onion, chopped
300 g carrots, chopped
1 tablespoon garam masala
¼ teaspoon hot chilli powder
¼ teaspoon ground turmeric
75 g dried red lentils, rinsed
400 g can chopped tomatoes
900 ml gluten free vegetable stock
410 g can green lentils, rinsed and
   drained
salt and freshly ground black
   pepper
6 tablespoons 0% fat natural Greek
   yogurt, to serve
3 tablespoons chopped fresh
   coriander, to garnish

This Indian-spiced soup contains two types of lentils — the red lentils break down to add thickness to the soup, while the green lentils are added after blending to give it more texture.

Spray a large lidded pan with the cooking spray and fry the onion for 3 minutes.

Add the carrots and the spices and cook for 1 minute, then tip in the red lentils, tomatoes and stock. Bring to the boil, cover and simmer for 20 minutes, or until the carrots are tender and the red lentils have broken down.

Blend the soup until smooth using a hand-held blender or a liquidiser. Add the green lentils to the pan and heat through for 2 minutes.

Serve the soup topped with a spoonful of the Greek yogurt and a scattering of coriander.

CHUNKY *Chickpea* & Chorizo **Soup**

 4 *ProPoints* values per serving
ProPoints values per recipe 15

 Serves 4
Preparation time 10 minutes
 Cooking time 15 minutes

75 g diced chorizo
1 onion, chopped
2 carrots, chopped
2 celery stalks, chopped
1 teaspoon ground coriander
½ teaspoon smoked paprika
2 tablespoons tomato purée
700 ml gluten free chicken stock
400 g can chickpeas, drained and
    rinsed
juice of 1 lemon
3 tablespoons chopped fresh flat
    leaf parsley
salt and freshly ground black
    pepper

A little chorizo goes a long way in this satisfying soup, packed full of hearty ingredients and bags of flavour.

Cook the chorizo for 2 minutes in a large lidded saucepan, until it starts to release its juices.

Add the onion, carrot and celery to the pan and cook, covered, for 5 minutes.

Mix in the spices and the tomato purée and cook for 1 minute before adding the stock, chickpeas and lemon juice.

Bring to the boil and cook, covered, for 15 minutes, or until the vegetables are tender.

Stir in the parsley and season to taste before serving.

Occasions

Posh Seafood LASAGNE

 ProPoints values per serving
ProPoints values per recipe 42

Serves 6
Preparation time 35 minutes
Cooking time 35 minutes

 Before cooking

500 g leeks, sliced and rinsed
150 ml vegetable stock
200 g young leaf spinach
200 g fat-free natural fromage frais
225 g skinless salmon fillet
350 g firm white fish fillet, skinned
2 bay leaves
40 g cornflour
600 ml skimmed milk
grated zest and juice of 1 lemon
3 sheets fresh lasagne
225 g cooked peeled king prawns
20 g freshly grated Parmesan cheese
salt and freshly ground black
    pepper

A prepare-ahead dish like lasagne is a great solution when you're entertaining friends or family, as you can just pop it in the oven and carry on socialising. This seafood version is a luxurious twist on a family favourite.

Place the leeks in a lidded pan with the stock. Season and cook for 15 minutes until soft. Drain.

Wilt the spinach in a lidded pan then press out the excess liquid, chop and combine with the fromage frais in a bowl. Season and set aside.

Add the salmon and white fish to a pan of boiling salted water with a bayleaf. Cook gently for 5 minutes until the fish starts to flake. Lift out on to a plate and break into large flakes.

Preheat the oven to Gas Mark 4/180°C/fan oven 160°C.

To make the white sauce, place the cornflour in a non-stick saucepan and gradually blend in the milk. Add the remaining bay leaf and bring to the boil, stirring until thickened. Add the lemon zest and juice, season and simmer the sauce for 5 minutes.

Cut the lasagne sheets in half, place in a bowl and cover with boiling water as per the packet instructions. Leave to soften for 5 minutes then drain.

To assemble the lasagne, spoon the drained leeks into the base of a 23 x 30 cm baking dish. Add half of the flaked fish and half of the prawns, drizzle with a quarter of the white sauce and then top with half the lasagne sheets.

Spread the spinach mixture over the lasagne sheets then add the rest of the fish and prawns. Top with the remaining lasagne sheets and pour the remaining white sauce all over the surface. Sprinkle with Parmesan. Bake for 30–35 minutes until the lasagne is bubbling and the top is golden brown. Leave to settle for 10 minutes before serving.

Sticky *Gingered* Salmon

A super-speedy supper dish for a busy day, when you don't want to do much cooking but still want a special meal.

 6 *ProPoints* values per serving
ProPoints values per recipe 12

Serves 2
Takes 10 minutes

1 piece stem ginger, plus
   1 tablespoon syrup from the jar
1 garlic clove, sliced
½ red chilli, sliced
juice of ½ lime
1 tablespoon gluten free dark
   soy sauce
2 x 100 g skinless salmon fillets
calorie controlled cooking spray
100 g asparagus tips
100 g baby corn, halved
150 g sugar snap peas
salt and freshly ground black
   pepper

Cut the stem ginger into matchsticks and place in a small bowl with the ginger syrup, garlic, chilli, lime juice, soy sauce and 2 tablespoons of cold water. Set aside.

Season the salmon and spray with the cooking spray. Add to a preheated non-stick frying pan, skinned side up, and cook for 2 minutes initially. Turn the salmon then pour the ginger sauce over and around it in the pan. Cook for a futher 3 minutes until the salmon is just cooked through.

Meanwhile, add the asparagus tips, baby corn and sugar snap peas to a pan of boiling water and cook for 3–4 minutes until just tender.

Drain the vegetables and divide between 2 warmed plates. Place the salmon on top of the vegetables and drizzle the sauce all over. Serve immediately.

Variation

Chicken will also work well in place of salmon in this recipe: use 2 x 150 g skinless chicken breast fillets. Cook the seasoned chicken for 5–6 minutes each side before adding the sauce and cooking for a further 3 minutes. The ***ProPoints*** values per serving will be 5.

Roast TURKEY & Stuffing with *Special* Cranberry Gravy

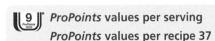 *ProPoints* values per serving
ProPoints values per recipe 37

Scrumptious sausage meat stuffing balls and delicious roasties accompany this simple roast turkey breast joint.

Serves 4
Preparation time 15 minutes
Cooking time 1 hour + resting

500 g turkey breast joint
calorie controlled cooking spray
400 g potatoes, chopped into
    chunky pieces and parboiled
40 g calorie controlled brown
    bread, torn
1 small onion, chopped roughly
1 tablespoon chopped fresh thyme
40 g dried apricots
4 Weight Watchers sausages, or
    similar
salt and freshly ground black
    pepper

For the gravy
4 heaped teaspoons chicken gravy
    granules
1 teaspoon chopped fresh thyme
250 ml boiling water
2 tablespoons red wine
2 tablespoons cranberry sauce

Preheat the oven to Gas Mark 5/190°C/fan oven 170°C.

Put the turkey breast joint in a large roasting tin and season. Spray with the cooking spray and place in the oven. After about 20 minutes add the potatoes to the roasting tin around the turkey and spray with the cooking spray.

Meanwhile, to make the stuffing balls, whizz the bread, onion, thyme and apricots together in a food processor (or use a hand-held blender) until finely chopped. Squeeze the sausage meat out of the skins, combine with the crumb mixture and season. Shape into 12 balls, cover and chill in the fridge.

After the turkey has cooked for 30 minutes, baste the joint and cover it with foil. Turn the potatoes over and add the stuffing balls to the roasting tin around the joint. Return to the oven for a further 30 minutes.

The turkey is cooked through when the juices run clear on piercing the thickest part of the joint with a skewer. Remove from the oven and leave to rest for 10 minutes.

To make the gravy, place the gravy granules in a jug with the thyme and mix in the boiling water, stirring until thickened. Add the red wine and the cranberry sauce, stirring to combine.

Remove the turkey skin before carving into thin slices. Serve 75 g sliced turkey breast and 3 stuffing balls per person, accompanied by the roast potatoes and gravy.

BACON Topped *Chicken* with Mustard *&* MOZZARELLA

 6 *ProPoints* values per serving
ProPoints values per recipe 24

 Serves 4
Preparation time 10 minutes
 Cooking time 20 minutes

3 courgettes, chopped roughly
250 g cherry tomatoes, halved
1 garlic clove, crushed
2 teaspoons chopped fresh thyme
calorie controlled cooking spray
125 g ball light mozzarella, drained
    and cubed
2 teaspoons grainy mustard
4 x 150 g skinless, boneless chicken
    breasts
4 bacon medallions
salt and freshly ground black
    pepper

Chicken is always a hugely popular choice and, with a filling of delicious melting cheese, this dish feels very luxurious. Serve with 150 g new potatoes per person and some baby corn, for an extra 3 *ProPoints* values per serving.

Preheat the oven to Gas Mark 6/200°C/fan oven 180°C.

Combine the courgettes, tomatoes, garlic and thyme in a roasting tin, season and spray with the cooking spray.

Mix the mozzarella and mustard together in a small bowl.

Cut a deep pocket in each chicken breast and stuff with the mozzarella mixture.

Nestle the chicken breasts in among the vegetables, spray with cooking spray, season and top each one with a bacon medallion.

Cook on the centre shelf of the oven for 20 minutes until the vegetables are tender, the chicken is cooked through and the cheesy filling is melting.

Serve straightaway, on warmed plates.

Sicilian MEATBALL & Orzo Bake

 ProPoints values per serving
ProPoints values per recipe 42

HC

Serves 4
Preparation time 20 minutes
Cooking time 35 minutes

2 slices Weight Watchers thick sliced
    wholemeal bread, or similar
3 tablespoons skimmed milk
2 garlic cloves, crushed
grated zest of ½ lemon
1 teaspoon fennel seeds
a pinch of chilli flakes
500 g extra lean pork mince
calorie controlled cooking spray
100 g dried orzo pasta
125 g ball light mozzarella, torn
20 g freshly grated Parmesan cheese
salt and freshly ground black
    pepper

For the sauce
1 onion, chopped
2 garlic cloves, crushed
1 red pepper, sliced
1 yellow pepper, sliced
300 ml chicken stock
400 g can chopped tomatoes

A melting cheese topping makes these meatballs very moreish. Serve this succulent and spicy meatball and orzo bake with a green salad.

Preheat the oven to Gas Mark 6/200°C/fan oven 180°C.

Whizz the bread to crumbs in a food processor, or use a hand-held blender. Set aside 2 tablespoons of breadcrumbs for the topping. Place the remainder in a mixing bowl with the milk to soften them, then add the garlic, lemon zest, fennel seeds, chilli flakes and pork mince. Mix well, and season.

Shape into 20 meatballs, place in a baking dish and spray with the cooking spray. Bake in the oven for 20 minutes until browned.

Meanwhile, make the sauce. Spray a large lidded saucepan with cooking spray and fry the onion for 2 minutes. Add the garlic, peppers and half of the stock. Season and cook, covered, for 5–7 minutes until softened and sweet.

While the sauce is cooking, add the orzo to a pan of boiling water and cook for 2 minutes less than the packet instructions suggest, as the pasta will continue to cook in the oven.

Add the rest of the stock and the chopped tomatoes to the sauce and simmer for 5 minutes.

Drain the orzo and add to the baking dish, around the meatballs, and pour the sauce over the top.

Scatter the mozzarella over the meatballs. Mix the Parmesan with the reserved breadcrumbs and sprinkle on top. Bake for 15 minutes until the topping is browned and the sauce is bubbling.

Sausage & MASH
with a Twist

 8 *ProPoints* values per serving
ProPoints values per recipe 31

 Serves 4
Preparation time 15 minutes
Cooking time 25 minutes

600 g potatoes, peeled and
    chopped
400 g celeriac, peeled and chopped
calorie controlled cooking spray
8 Weight Watchers sausages,
    or similar
2 red onions, sliced thinly
1 tablespoon white wine vinegar
100 ml dry or medium white wine
4 teaspoons redcurrant jelly
1 tablespoon chopped fresh
    rosemary, or 1 teaspoon dried
    rosemary
100 ml chicken stock
6 tablespoons skimmed milk
salt and freshly ground black
    pepper

Glam up an everyday favourite by adding celeriac to regular mashed potato, and serving with a white wine sauce. Try with some sugar snap peas; they go well with this dish.

Add the potatoes and celeriac to a pan of boiling water. Cook for 15–20 minutes until tender.

Meanwhile, spray a non-stick frying pan with the cooking spray. Add the sausages and cook over a medium heat for 8 minutes, turning regularly. Add the red onions, and continue to cook, stirring the pan contents occasionally, for another 8 minutes.

Increase the heat under the frying pan and add the vinegar, which should bubble and evaporate within a few seconds. Add the wine, redcurrant jelly and rosemary and cook for about 1 minute.

Add the stock to the pan, bring the sauce to the boil and simmer for 3 minutes, turning the sausages in the sauce to glaze them.

Drain the potatoes and celeriac and return to the pan. Add the skimmed milk, season and mash until smooth.

Serve the mash, sausages and sauce on warmed plates.

 Variation

For a vegetarian variation, switch to Quorn sausages and vegetable stock, for 8 *ProPoints* values per serving. Quorn sausages don't need as long to cook, so simply cook them with the onions for 8 minutes, without pre-browning.

Cook's tip Celeriac is a rather ugly looking vegetable, but don't be put off! With a mild celery-like flavour, it adds a really tasty twist to straightforward mash. Rather than struggling to prepare it using a vegetable peeler, simply slice off the thick outside layer with a kitchen knife.

Steaks Topped with *Creamy* MUSHROOM Gratin

6 *ProPoints* values per serving
ProPoints values per recipe 24

GF

LC

Serves 4
Preparation time 15 minutes
Cooking time 35 minutes

4 x 100 g medallion steaks
1.25 kg butternut squash, peeled
calorie controlled cooking spray
250 g mixed mushrooms, sliced
1 egg yolk
2 tablespoons Weight Watchers
    crème fraîche, or similar
¼ teaspoon Dijon mustard
1 teaspoon chopped fresh tarragon,
    or ½ teaspoon dried tarragon
15 g freshly grated Parmesan cheese
salt and freshly ground black
    pepper

Proper steak and chips but with a delicious mushroom gratin topping to add a little luxury. Serve with a heap of steamed broccoli.

Preheat the oven to Gas Mark 6/200°C/fan oven 180°C and preheat a baking tray on the centre shelf. Remove the steaks from the fridge.

Cut the butternut squash into 2 cm wide chips. Spray the hot tray with the cooking spray, add the butternut squash chips, season them and spray with extra cooking spray. Cook in the oven for 30 minutes, turning halfway through, until tender and starting to caramelise.

While the chips are cooking, prepare the mushroom gratin topping. Spray a frying pan with the cooking spray and fry the mushrooms for 4–5 minutes until tender. Tip out on to a plate to cool, and wipe out the pan with kitchen paper.

Combine the egg yolk, crème fraîche, mustard and tarragon in a bowl, and season. Stir in the cooled mushrooms.

About 10 minutes before the butternut chips are ready, season the steaks. Pan-fry for 2–3 minutes each side, depending on the thickness of the steaks. Preheat the grill while the steaks are cooking. Spoon the mushroom gratin topping on top of the steaks and sprinkle with the Parmesan cheese.

Pop the pan under the grill, protecting the handle from the heat. Grill the steaks for 3 minutes, or until the gratin topping is glazed. Serve with the butternut squash chips.

Variation

The mushroom gratin topping is also delicious on pork steaks: substitute 4 x 125 g lean pork loin steaks for the medallion steaks. Pan-fry the pork steaks for 4 minutes each side before adding the mushroom gratin topping. The ***ProPoints*** values per serving will be 7.

Sunday BEST Beef with Honey Roasted Parsnips

9 *ProPoints* values per serving
ProPoints values per recipe 37

Serves 4
Preparation time 15 minutes
Cooking time 1 hour 10 minutes + resting

1 red onion, cut into wedges
1 white onion, cut into wedges
700 g extra lean beef roasting joint
calorie controlled cooking spray
4 medium parsnips, peeled
juice of 1 orange
3 teaspoons honey
½ teaspoon ground ginger
150 ml red wine
25 g plain flour
500 ml beef stock
salt and freshly ground black pepper

A Sunday roast is a great family tradition. Serve with the usual classic vegetable accompaniments, such as steamed or boiled carrots and cabbage, for no extra *ProPoints* values.

Preheat the oven to Gas Mark 5/190°C/fan oven 170°C.

Place the onion wedges in a small roasting tin and nestle the beef joint on top. Season the beef and spray with the cooking spray. Roast in the oven for 30 minutes initially.

While the beef is cooking, cut the parsnips into chunky wedges and parboil for 5 minutes. Drain and spray with the cooking spray and tip into a shallow roasting tray.

When the 30 minutes are up, add the tray of parsnips to the oven and cook both beef and parsnips for 30 minutes.

Place the orange juice, honey and ground ginger in a small pan, season and boil for 5 minutes to reduce to a thicker glaze.

After the 30 minutes, remove the beef from the oven and transfer to a warmed plate. Cover with foil and leave to rest for 10 minutes. Drizzle the honey glaze over the parsnips and return them to the oven for 5–10 minutes while the beef is resting, until sticky and golden.

Pour the red wine into the beef roasting tin, stir around to loosen the onions and caramelised juices, then tip the onions and wine into a saucepan. Sprinkle in the flour and then gradually add the stock. Bring to the boil, stirring, and leave to simmer for 5 minutes.

Carve the beef into thin slices and serve 110 g beef per person, accompanied by the honey roasted parsnips and red wine gravy.

SMOKED *Paprika* BEEF Stew

 Serves 4
Preparation time 20 minutes
 Cooking time 1½ hours

 500 g lean braising steak, cubed
calorie controlled cooking spray
 2 onions, sliced
2 garlic cloves, crushed
½ tablespoon smoked paprika
400 g can chopped tomatoes
300 ml gluten free beef stock
1 red pepper, sliced
1 green pepper, sliced
410 g can butter beans, rinsed and
  drained
salt and freshly ground black
  pepper

This comforting stew is wonderful served with mashed potato: 200 g per person, mashed without adding fat, will be an extra 4 *ProPoints* values per serving.

Preheat the oven to Gas Mark 2/150°C/fan oven 130°C.

Season the steak and spray a lidded ovenproof casserole with the cooking spray. Brown the steak in two batches, removing the meat to a plate as it is browned.

Spray the casserole with a little more cooking spray and cook the onions for 5 minutes. Stir in the garlic and smoked paprika and cook for 1 minute, then add the tomatoes, beef stock and browned beef. Season the stew, bring to a simmer, then cover and cook in the oven for 1 hour.

Stir the peppers and butter beans into the stew, pushing them down into the liquid, then replace the lid and cook for a further 30 minutes, or until the meat is tender.

Gorgeous Pesto Lamb

  ProPoints values per serving
ProPoints values per recipe 29

 Serves 4
Takes 15 minutes

4 x 100 g lean lamb leg steaks
3 tablespoons pesto
250 g cherry tomatoes, halved
2 garlic cloves, crushed
calorie controlled cooking spray
250 g fine green beans, halved
400 g can flageolet beans
juice of ½ lemon
salt and freshly ground black
   pepper

Food for friends needn't take hours to prepare in order to impress! This beauty of a lamb dish can be on the table in just 15 minutes from scratch. Serve with a spinach salad.

Preheat the grill. Place the lamb steaks on a shallow baking tray, season, and spread 1 tablespoon of pesto between the 4 steaks.

Combine the tomatoes with the garlic in a bowl, season and spray with the cooking spray. Tip onto the tray with the lamb.

Grill the lamb and tomatoes for 4 minutes initially.

Meanwhile, add the green beans to a pan of boiling water and cook for 5–6 minutes, or until just tender. Tip the flageolet beans and their canning liquid into another saucepan and heat through gently.

Turn the lamb steaks and spread with another tablespoon of pesto. Cook the lamb and tomatoes for a further 4 minutes.

Drain the flageolet beans and rinse with hot water from the kettle. Drain the green beans and tip both types of bean back into one of the pans. Mix with the remaining tablespoon of pesto and the lemon juice.

Divide the bean mixture between 4 warmed plates and serve topped with the garlic tomatoes and the lamb. Drizzle the cooking juices from the tray over the lamb just before serving.

Variation

If you love chicken, replace the lamb steaks with 4 x 150 g skinless chicken breast fillets (they will take a little longer to cook). Grill the plain chicken breasts on their own for 3 minutes each side, then add the tomatoes to the tray and drizzle the chicken with pesto and continue as above, cooking for a further 4 minutes each side. The **ProPoints** values per serving will be 6.

STILTON & Leek Tartlets

4 ProPoints values per serving
ProPoints values per recipe 24

Serves 6
Preparation time 25 minutes

Cooking time 15 minutes

calorie controlled cooking spray
400 g leeks, sliced
½ teaspoon dried sage
100 ml vegetable stock
3 x 45 g sheets filo pastry measuring
    50 x 24 cm, defrosted if frozen
75 g vegetarian Stilton cheese,
    crumbled
2 eggs
150 ml skimmed milk
salt and freshly ground black
    pepper

Serve these gorgeous little tartlets with 150 g baby new potatoes per person, for an additional 3 **ProPoints** values per serving. Accompany with either a mixed salad, or mange tout and baby corn, depending on the season.

Preheat the oven to Gas Mark 4/180°C/fan oven 160°C.

Spray a lidded saucepan with the cooking spray and fry the leeks for 2 minutes. Add the sage and stock, and season. Cook, covered, for 15 minutes, stirring occasionally, until the leeks are tender and the liquid has evaporated.

Meanwhile, prepare the tart cases. Spray 6 Yorkshire pudding tins with the cooking spray and place on a baking tray.

Cut the filo sheets in half and stack up as 6 squares. Working with one square at a time, spray with the cooking spray then fold it into quarters. Press this smaller layered square of filo into the prepared tin, with the points overhanging the edges. Repeat with the remaining filo squares to make a total of 6 tart cases, and spray each one with extra cooking spray.

Divide the cooked leeks between the tart cases and crumble in the Stilton cheese.

Beat the eggs and milk, season and pour over the filling. Bake on the centre shelf of the oven for 15 minutes until the filling is just set and the pastry is golden and crisp.

Serve the tartlets warm from the oven.

Cook's tip To avoid spilling the egg mixture when transferring the filled tarts to the oven, place the tray on the oven shelf first and then pour in the egg mixture.

Mexican *Tamale* Pie

 ProPoints values per serving
ProPoints values per recipe 46

 Serves 6
Preparation time 15 minutes
 Cooking time 25 minutes

calorie controlled cooking spray
1 onion, chopped
1 red pepper, chopped
1 yellow pepper, chopped
1 courgette, chopped
2 garlic cloves, crushed
1 teaspoon ground cumin
¼ teaspoon hot chilli powder
400 g can chopped tomatoes
420 g can beans in chilli sauce
198 g can sweetcorn

For the tamale topping
125 g self-raising flour
1 teaspoon baking powder
100 g fine cornmeal or polenta
1 egg
250 ml skimmed milk
50 g low fat spread, melted
salt and freshly ground black
　　pepper

Traditional Mexican tamales combine spiced minced meat with a cornmeal dough, wrapped in corn husks and then steamed. These flavours provide the inspiration for this recipe, which has a light cornbread layer baked on top of a layer of chilli beans and vegetables — beautiful!

Preheat the oven to Gas Mark 4/180°C/fan oven 160°C.

Spray a large lidded pan with the cooking spray and fry the onion for 2 minutes before adding the peppers, courgette and garlic. Cook for 3 minutes, stirring.

Add the spices and cook for 1 minute then tip in the tomatoes, beans in chilli sauce and sweetcorn. Simmer for 10 minutes then tip into a 23 cm diameter baking dish.

To make the tamale topping, sift the flour, baking powder and a pinch of salt into a mixing bowl then stir in the cornmeal or polenta.

Mix the egg, milk and melted low fat spread together with a grinding of black pepper then stir the wet ingredients into the dry. Spoon the tamale topping on top of the vegetable and bean mixture in the dish, and spread out to the edges.

Bake in the oven for about 25 minutes until the topping is risen, firm and golden brown.

Vegetarian STROGANOFF

 **8** *ProPoints* values per serving
ProPoints values per recipe 34

 Serves 4
Takes 20 minutes

 calorie controlled cooking spray

 4 shallots, sliced
2 garlic cloves, crushed

 250 g mushrooms, sliced thickly
300 ml vegetable stock
350 g Quorn meat-free chicken
   pieces
1 teaspoon grainy mustard
200 g 0% fat natural Greek yogurt
1 tablespoon chopped fresh
   tarragon
grated zest of ½ lemon
salt and freshly ground black
   pepper
200 g dried brown rice or
   wholewheat pasta, cooked
   according to the packet
   instructions, to serve

This creamy stroganoff is really good served with some green beans on the side.

Spray a non-stick frying pan with the cooking spray and fry the shallots for 2 minutes. Add the garlic, mushrooms and 4 tablespoons of the stock and cook for 3 minutes, stirring.

Pour the rest of the stock into the pan and add the Quorn pieces. Season, and bubble the stroganoff for 5 minutes.

Remove the pan from the heat and leave to cool for 5 minutes.

Stir the mustard and yogurt into the stroganoff, off the heat. If you add the yogurt to the sauce when it is straight off the boil, the yogurt will split and the sauce will curdle; by allowing it to cool a little first, you should end up with a smooth, creamy sauce, but without making the whole dish too cold.

Sprinkle the tarragon and lemon zest over the stroganoff before serving with the rice or pasta.

Variation

If you fancy a bit of meat you can replace the Quorn pieces with 450 g cubed skinless chicken breast. Start by browning the chicken in calorie controlled cooking spray, remove to a plate and then carry on with the recipe as above. The **ProPoints** values per serving will be 9.

Cook's tip If you're not on a Filling & Healthy day, you can stabilise the yogurt to prevent it from curdling by adding 1 tablespoon cornflour mixed with 2 tablespoons of cold water. Stir into the yogurt before adding it to the sauce. The *ProPoints* values per serving will be 9.

Fakeaways

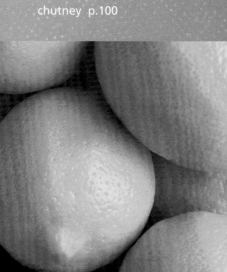

Stir-fried *Chicken* in OYSTER Sauce

 9 *ProPoints* values per serving
ProPoints values per recipe 17

 Serves 2
Takes 20 minutes

250 g chicken mini fillets, cubed
    or skinless chicken breast, cubed
calorie controlled cooking spray
1 onion, sliced
100 g broccoli, cut into small florets
2 garlic cloves, sliced
2 cm fresh root ginger, shredded
100 g mushrooms, quartered
4 tablespoons oyster sauce
salt and freshly ground black
    pepper
80 g dried noodles, cooked
    according to the packet
    instructions, to serve

**A tempting stir-fry that makes a great midweek supper —
it's even quicker than ordering a takeaway!**

Season the chicken and spray a wok or non-stick frying pan with the cooking spray. Fry the chicken over a high heat for 3 minutes until browned, then remove to a plate.

Stir-fry the onion for 2 minutes, or until starting to brown, then add the broccoli, garlic, ginger, mushrooms and 4 tablespoons of water. Stir-fry for 3 minutes, adding another 2 tablespoons of water if needed, to cook the vegetables through.

Return the chicken to the wok or frying pan. Mix the oyster sauce with 3 tablespoons of water and add to the pan. Cook for 2 minutes, stirring to mix well.

Serve immediately with the noodles.

 Variation

Vegetarians can replace the cubed chicken breast with the same weight of Quorn Chicken Style Pieces, and substitute hoisin sauce for the oyster sauce. The ***ProPoints*** values per serving will be 9.

Cook's tips Steam-frying, by adding a little water to the stir-fry pan, is a great method for ensuring that vegetables cook through quickly without adding any fat. Only add a little water at a time, however, or the vegetables will boil rather than steam-fry.

If you want a lower carb version of this dish, just serve without the noodles.

Crispy CHICKEN with FRIES & Coleslaw

 10 *ProPoints* values per serving
ProPoints values per recipe 39

 Serves 4

Preparation time 30 minutes +
    marinating
Cooking time 30 minutes

4 x 125 g skinless chicken breast
    fillets
150 g fat-free natural yogurt
grated zest and juice of ½ lemon
1 garlic clove, crushed
700 g potatoes, unpeeled, cut into
    chips
½ vegetable stock cube
40 g Weight Watchers thick sliced
    wholemeal bread, or similar
30 g cornflakes
calorie controlled cooking spray
salt and freshly ground black
    pepper

For the coleslaw
200 g white cabbage, shredded
1 large carrot, grated coarsely
1 small shallot, sliced finely
2 tablespoons light mayonnaise
100 g fat-free natural yogurt

This recipe just goes to show that you can still enjoy takeaway-style food and keep within your *ProPoints* values allowance.

Ahead of time, marinate the chicken to tenderise and add extra flavour. Slash the chicken breasts to allow the flavours to permeate. Mix together the yogurt, lemon zest and juice and garlic. Season and pour over the chicken in a plastic food bag. Seal tightly so that the marinade is in close contact with the meat. Marinate in the fridge for at least 2 hours, or overnight.

When you are ready to cook, preheat the oven to Gas Mark 7/220°C/ fan oven 200°C, and place a baking tray in the oven to preheat.

Add the potato chips and the crumbled stock cube to a pan of boiling water. Bring back to the boil and cook for 5 minutes.

Meanwhile, whizz the bread and cornflakes together with some salt and black pepper to make the crumb coating, and tip it out into a shallow dish. Shake the marinade off the chicken and press the crumb coating all over the meat.

Drain the potato chips and shake gently in the pan to slightly roughen the edges. Spray the hot tray with the cooking spray. Tip the potato chips on to the tray and spray with extra cooking spray. Cook in the oven for 15 minutes, on the top shelf.

To make the coleslaw, combine the cabbage, carrot and shallot in a mixing bowl. Season to taste and stir in the mayonnaise and yogurt to coat evenly.

Stir the chips around to cook evenly and move the tray to the centre shelf. Place the coated chicken breasts on a rack on a baking tray and place on the top shelf. Cook for 15 minutes until the chips are golden brown and the chicken is crisp and cooked through.

Serve with the coleslaw.

Tandoori CHICKEN
with Green Chutney

 9 *ProPoints* values per serving
ProPoints values per recipe 38

 Serves 4

Preparation time 20 minutes +
   marinating

 Cooking time 20 minutes

 GF

 HC

1 onion, chopped roughly

½ green chilli, chopped roughly

2 garlic cloves

2 cm fresh root ginger, sliced

2 teaspoons garam masala

½ teaspoon ground turmeric

calorie controlled cooking spray

3 tablespoons tomato purée

200 g fat-free natural yogurt

450 g cubed skinless chicken breast

400 g can chopped tomatoes

200 ml gluten free chicken stock

salt and freshly ground black
   pepper

200 g dried brown rice, cooked
   according to the packet
   instructions, to serve

For the green chutney

4 tablespoons chopped fresh
   coriander

2 tablespoons chopped fresh mint

½ green chilli

juice of ½ lime

2 tablespoons fat-free natural
   yogurt

A refreshing coriander and mint chutney adds a zing to this flavoursome curry. Don't be put off by the long list of ingredients — the first eight are used to make a curry paste that forms the basis of both the chicken marinade and the curry sauce.

Ahead of time, place the onion, chilli, garlic, ginger and spices in a small food processor (or use a hand-held blender) with 4 tablespoons of water. Season and blitz to a paste.

Spray a non-stick frying pan with the cooking spray and fry the paste for 4–5 minutes, stirring, until the paste is quite dry and aromatic. Add the tomato purée and cook for 1 minute then tip on to a plate to cool.

Combine half of the curry paste with the yogurt in a non-reactive container, stir in the chicken, cover and marinate for at least 2 hours, or overnight. Chill the rest of the curry paste ready to make the sauce.

When ready to cook, preheat the grill to high. Tip the reserved curry paste into a lidded saucepan and add the chopped tomatoes and chicken stock. Simmer, covered, for 15 minutes.

Spread the marinated chicken out in a single layer on a foil-lined tray and grill for about 10 minutes until the chicken is cooked through and starting to char at the edges. Tip the tandoori chicken into the curry sauce and simmer for 3–4 minutes.

Make the green chutney by blitzing the ingredients together in a small food processor (or use a hand-held blender). Serve the chutney drizzled over the curry, accompanied by the rice.

Cook's tips The curry, without the chutney or rice, is suitable for freezing for up to 3 months.

For a lower carb dish, serve without the rice.

CAESAR *Turkey* Burgers

 ProPoints values per serving
ProPoints values per recipe 33

Serves 4
Takes 25 minutes

calorie controlled cooking spray
3 shallots, chopped finely
2 garlic cloves, crushed
40 g wholemeal breadcrumbs
3 tablespoons skimmed milk
grated zest of ½ lemon
25 g freshly grated Parmesan cheese
500 g turkey breast mince
salt and freshly ground black
    pepper

To serve
2 tablespoons low fat Caesar
    dressing
3 tablespoons 0% fat natural Greek
    yogurt
4 brown sandwich thins
3 tomatoes, sliced
75 g Romaine lettuce, shredded

Burgers are a great family favourite, and these scrummy turkey burgers are finished off with salad and a luscious Caesar-style sauce.

Spray a frying pan with the cooking spray and soften the shallot and garlic for 3 minutes, without browning.

Combine the breadcrumbs, milk, lemon zest, Parmesan and the shallot mixture, then mix with the turkey mince. Season to taste.

Shape into 4 large burgers and preheat the grill.

Spray the burgers with the cooking spray and grill for 12–15 minutes until cooked through, turning halfway.

Meanwhile, combine the Caesar dressing and yogurt in a bowl for the sauce.

Lightly toast the sandwich thins and split them open. Add some sliced tomato, lettuce, a burger and a dollop of sauce. Serve immediately.

Tex-Mex Turkey

7 *ProPoints* values per serving
ProPoints values per recipe 30

Serves 4
Preparation time 15 minutes
Cooking time 20 minutes

 Turkey mixture only

calorie controlled cooking spray
1 red onion, chopped roughly
1 red pepper, chopped roughly
1 courgette, chopped roughly
1 tablespoon ground cumin
1 teaspoon smoked paprika
¼ teaspoon chilli powder
2 garlic cloves, crushed
500 g cubed turkey breast
400 g can chopped tomatoes
150 ml gluten free chicken stock
198 g can sweetcorn, drained
4 tablespoons Weight Watchers
   crème fraîche, or similar
60 g tortilla chips, crushed (ensure
   gluten free)
salt and freshly ground black
   pepper

Get all the flavours of Tex-Mex tacos, but without the *ProPoints* values, with this ace Friday night dinner.

Spray a lidded flameproof casserole with the cooking spray. Fry the onion, pepper and courgette over a high heat for 3 minutes, stirring.

Add the spices, garlic and turkey, and cook for 2 minutes before adding the tomatoes, stock and sweetcorn. Season and simmer, covered, for 20 minutes.

Serve the turkey mixture ladled into bowls, topped with a spoonful of crème fraîche and the crushed tortilla chips.

 Variations
Vegetarians can replace the turkey breast with a 350 g packet of Quorn Chicken Style Pieces, and use vegetable rather than chicken stock. The *ProPoints* values per serving will be 7. Alternatively, use a 400 g can drained kidney beans, for 6 *ProPoints* values per serving.

CHINESE *Duck* Wraps

 ProPoints values per serving
ProPoints values per recipe 35

 Serves 4
Preparation time 15 minutes
Cooking time 20 minutes + 1 hour resting

2 x 140 g skinless duck breasts
2 tablespoons dark soy sauce
2 teaspoons Chinese five spice powder
4 cm fresh root ginger, sliced

To serve
8 Weight Watchers tortillas, or similar
4 tablespoons plum or hoisin sauce
1 Little Gem lettuce, separated into leaves
175 g cucumber, cut into matchsticks
3 spring onions, shredded
150 g beansprouts, rinsed

A main meal version of the ever-popular Chinese duck pancakes to make at home.

Place the duck breasts in a medium lidded pan with the soy sauce, Chinese five spice powder, ginger, and about 500 ml cold water (enough to cover the duck). Bring to the boil with the lid on. Reduce the heat to the lowest setting and simmer for 20 minutes, turning the duck breasts over halfway through.

Remove from the heat and leave to stand for 1 hour to finish cooking and infuse with flavour.

Remove the duck from the cooking liquor (reserve 4 tablespoons). Shred the meat and mix with the reserved cooking liquor.

When ready to serve, gently reheat the shredded duck, either in a lidded saucepan or in the microwave. Warm the tortilla wraps according to the packet instructions.

Let everyone assemble their own wraps: drizzle a wrap with a little plum or hoisin sauce, add a couple of lettuce leaves and then pile on the shredded cucumber, spring onions, beansprouts and duck.

Cook's tip You can easily cook and shred the duck a day ahead. Cover and store it in the fridge, and then reheat it when ready to serve.

Beef Keema Dhansak & Fresh MANGO CHUTNEY

 ProPoints values per serving
ProPoints values per recipe 27

Serves 6
Preparation time 20 minutes
Cooking time 30 minutes

✱ Curry only

♥ calorie controlled cooking spray
500 g extra lean beef mince

 1 onion, chopped finely
1½ tablespoons garam masala

 ½ teaspoon chilli powder

 ½ teaspoon ground turmeric
2 garlic cloves, crushed
400 g can chopped tomatoes
100 g dried red lentils, rinsed
400 ml gluten free beef stock
100 g young leaf spinach
salt and freshly ground black
    pepper

For the fresh mango chutney
1 large ripe mango, peeled and
    chopped finely
½ red chilli, chopped finely
grated zest and juice of ½ lime
3 tablespoons chopped fresh
    coriander

The term 'dhansak' signifies a hot, sweet and sour dish with lentils, and also often containing greens. This fragrant curry is served with a sweet fresh mango and coriander relish.

Spray a large flameproof lidded casserole with the cooking spray. Brown the mince and onion together for 5 minutes over a high heat, stirring frequently to break the mince up.

Add the spices and garlic and cook for 2 minutes.

Mix in the tomatoes, rinsed lentils and stock. Bring to the boil, cover and simmer for 25 minutes until the lentils are soft.

Stir in the spinach, adjust the seasoning to taste and cook for a further 5 minutes.

While the curry is cooking, simply combine the mango chutney ingredients in a bowl and set aside for the flavours to infuse.

Ladle the curry into warmed bowls and serve topped with the fresh mango chutney.

MASSAMAN *Beef* CURRY

ProPoints values per serving
ProPoints values per recipe 41

 GF

Serves 4
Takes 30 minutes

 LC

calorie controlled cooking spray
4 shallots, sliced
400 g potatoes, peeled and cubed
1 teaspoon curry powder
2 tablespoons red Thai curry paste
 (ensure gluten free)
200 ml light coconut milk
1 tablespoon Thai fish sauce (ensure
 gluten free)
400 ml gluten free beef stock
1 cinnamon stick
100 g fine green beans, halved
300 g lean beef escalopes, cut into
 strips

To garnish
25 g peanuts, chopped finely
½ red chilli, sliced finely

This classic Thai curry gains its richness from the use of coconut milk. Light coconut milk is used in this recipe to reduce the *ProPoints* values — but without sacrificing too much flavour.

Spray a large lidded saucepan with the cooking spray and fry the shallots for 2 minutes.

Add the potatoes, curry powder and Thai curry paste and cook, stirring, for 1 minute.

Pour in the coconut milk, fish sauce and beef stock. Add the cinnamon stick and simmer, covered, for 10 minutes.

Add the green beans to the pan and cook for a further 5 minutes before adding the beef. Cook gently for 3 minutes or until the beef is just cooked through but still tender. Remove the cinnamon stick.

Ladle the curry into bowls and sprinkle the chopped peanuts and chilli on top as a garnish.

Cook's tip Beef escalopes are sliced very thinly, so you need to cook the meat quickly to make sure that the beef doesn't turn rubbery.

Lamb SHAWARMA Stuffed Pittas

 ProPoints values per serving
ProPoints values per recipe 41

Serves 4
Preparation time 20 minutes +
  marinating
Cooking time 10 minutes

400 g lean lamb leg steaks, cubed
100 g fat-free natural yogurt
grated zest and juice of ½ lemon
1 tablespoon cider vinegar
4 cardamom pods, crushed
¼ teaspoon ground allspice
½ teaspoon ground cumin
1 garlic clove, crushed
salt and freshly ground black
  pepper

To serve
100 g fat-free natural yogurt
1 tablespoon tahini
1 small garlic clove, crushed
3 tomatoes, chopped roughly
100 g cucumber, chopped roughly
3 pickled cucumbers, sliced
4 wholemeal pittas

A favourite choice on a night out, you can still enjoy shawarma at home with this succulent lower **ProPoints** values version. The tahini-yogurt sauce adds a characteristic flavour of the Middle East.

Ahead of time, marinate the lamb. Combine the yogurt, lemon zest and juice, vinegar, spices and garlic. Season and mix with the lamb. Cover and marinate for at least 2 hours, or overnight.

When ready to cook, preheat the grill to a high setting.

Shake the marinade off the pieces of lamb and spread out on a foil-lined tray. Grill for 8–10 minutes until the lamb is cooked through and starting to char at the edges.

Meanwhile, stir the yogurt, tahini and garlic together to make the sauce, then combine the tomatoes, cucumber and pickled cucumbers in a separate bowl. Lightly toast the pittas under the grill and split them open.

Stuff the pittas with the lamb and salad, and drizzle generously with the tahini-yogurt sauce.

Variation
You can replace the lamb with 450 g cubed skinless chicken breast. The **ProPoints** values per serving will be 8.

Cook's tip Tahini is a sesame paste that is used a lot in Middle Eastern cooking. It's a key flavour in houmous.

SESAME *Prawns* with Sweet & SOUR Noodles

 ProPoints values per serving
ProPoints values per recipe 19

A Chinese-style dish with lightly battered crispy sesame-coated prawns served on top of a pile of vegetable noodles in a sweet-sour sauce.

Serves 2
Takes 25 minutes

3 tablespoons sesame seeds
1 egg white
1 teaspoon cornflour
225 g raw peeled tiger prawns, de-veined
calorie controlled cooking spray
75 g dried wholewheat egg noodles
300 g packet prepared stir-fry vegetables
1 garlic clove, sliced
salt and freshly ground black pepper

For the sauce
½ tablespoon cornflour
2 tablespoons soy sauce
juice of ½ lemon
2 teaspoons clear honey
2 cm fresh root ginger, grated

Toast the sesame seeds in a wok or non-stick frying pan until golden, then tip on to a plate to cool.

In a small bowl, lightly beat the egg white until foamy. Season the cornflour in a separate bowl and mix with the toasted sesame seeds. Dip each prawn in the egg white and allow the excess to drip off, then roll in the sesame seed mixture to coat. Place on a baking tray and spray with the cooking spray. Preheat the grill.

Make the sauce by blending the cornflour with the soy sauce, lemon juice and honey, then add 150 ml cold water and the ginger, and set aside.

Cook the noodles according to the packet instructions, drain and refresh in cold water.

Pop the sesame prawns under the grill and cook for 5 minutes until the prawns are starting to curl and have changed from translucent grey to opaque pink.

While the prawns are cooking, spray the wok or non-stick frying pan with the cooking spray. Stir-fry the vegetables and garlic for 3 minutes. Add the drained noodles, give the sauce a stir and then pour into the wok or pan. Cook for 1 minute, stirring to mix everything well and coat in the sauce, which will thicken as it cooks.

Divide the vegetable noodles between 2 bowls and serve the sesame prawns on top.

Keralan *Coconut* FISH Curry

5 *ProPoints* values per serving
ProPoints values per recipe 19

 Serves 4
Takes 20 minutes

1 small onion, chopped roughly
3 garlic cloves
2 cm fresh root ginger, sliced
1 tablespoon hot curry powder
   e.g. Madras
grated zest and juice of ½ lime
300 ml light coconut milk
calorie controlled cooking spray
450 g firm white fish fillets, cubed
200 g cherry tomatoes, halved
100 g young leaf spinach
salt and freshly ground black
   pepper

Coconut is a classic ingredient in southern Indian cooking, and light coconut milk forms the basis of the sauce in this fish curry. To mop up the luscious sauce, serve with 40 g dried brown rice per person, cooked according to the packet instructions, or a mini naan bread — both will add an extra 4 *ProPoints* values per serving.

Place the onion, garlic, ginger, curry powder, lime zest and juice in a small food processor with 2 tablespoons of the coconut milk and whiz to a paste (or use a hand-held blender).

Spray a non-stick saucepan with the cooking spray and tip in the spice paste. Fry for 4–5 minutes to cook out the raw flavours.

Add the fish to the pan and turn gently to coat in the spice paste.

Pour the rest of the coconut milk into the pan and stir in the tomatoes. Bring to the boil and simmer gently for 5 minutes until the fish is cooked but not falling apart.

Remove from the heat and stir in the spinach, to wilt in the heat of the sauce. Adjust the seasoning to taste.

Ladle into warmed bowls to serve.

Cook's tip You'll have 100 ml coconut milk left over from a 400 ml can at the end of this recipe, but it can be frozen for use in another recipe (such as a Thai curry).

Fish Fingers, CHIPS & Pea Purée

 10 *ProPoints* values per serving
ProPoints values per recipe 42

 Serves 4
Preparation time 15 minutes
 Cooking time 25 minutes

750 g baking potatoes, peeled and
    cut into thin chips
½ vegetable stock cube
calorie controlled cooking spray
200 g skinless salmon fillets
300 g skinless haddock fillets
1 egg
50 g fresh breadcrumbs made from
    calorie controlled brown bread
200 g frozen peas
3 tablespoons hot vegetable stock
50 g fat-free natural fromage frais
salt and freshly ground black
    pepper

This is bound to be a family favourite, and the pea purée makes a lovely dipping sauce for the fish fingers and chips.

Preheat the oven to Gas Mark 7/220°C/fan oven 200°C and place a large tray on the top shelf to preheat.

Add the potato chips and stock cube to a large pan of boiling water. Bring back to the boil and cook for 3 minutes. Drain the chips and shake gently in the pan to slightly roughen up the edges. Spray the hot tray with the cooking spray and tip the chips out to make an even layer on the tray. Spray with extra cooking spray. Cook in the oven for 10 minutes.

Meanwhile, cut the fish into chunky strips. Beat the egg in a shallow bowl with 1 tablespoon of water and season. Spread the breadcrumbs out on a plate. Dip the fish strips into the egg and then roll in the crumbs to coat. Add to the tray of chips and cook for 10 minutes until crisp and golden.

Cook the frozen peas according to the packet instructions. Tip into a food processor (or use a hand-held blender) with the stock. Blitz to a purée and then blend in the fromage frais. Check the seasoning.

Pour the pea purée into 4 small bowls and serve with the fish fingers and chips.

Variation

For more traditional fish fingers, skip the salmon and use a total of 500 g skinless haddock fillets, cut into strips. The *ProPoints* values per serving will be 9.

Ham & Mushroom PANZEROTTI

9 *ProPoints* values per serving
ProPoints values per recipe 37

 Serves 4
Preparation time 20 minutes
Cooking time 15–20 minutes

calorie controlled cooking spray
200 g button mushrooms, quartered
1 garlic clove, crushed
250 g fresh or defrosted pizza
    dough
200 g tomato and herb pizza sauce
150 g wafer thin ham, torn roughly
2 tablespoons chopped fresh basil,
    plus extra leaves to garnish
125 g ball light mozzarella, drained
    and cubed
25 g grated fresh Parmesan cheese
salt and freshly ground black
    pepper

Similar to a calzone, but closer in size to a Cornish pasty, these stuffed pizza pies can hold all manner of fillings (see below for suggestions). Serve with a big mixed salad.

Preheat the oven to Gas Mark 6/200°C/fan oven 180°C.

Spray a non-stick frying pan with the cooking spray, add the mushrooms, garlic, some salt and black pepper, and a splash of water to get them started. Cook for 5 minutes until the mushrooms are tender and any liquid has evaporated. Tip out on to a plate to cool.

Divide the pizza dough into 4 and roll each piece out to a 18 cm circle. Transfer to a large baking tray. Spread each one with a tablespoon of pizza sauce then pile up the mushrooms, ham, basil, mozzarella and Parmesan in the centre.

Bring the pizza dough up over the filling in a pasty shape, and pinch the edges together to seal. Flip over so that the panzerotti are seam-side down on the tray. Bake for 15–20 minutes until the dough is crisp and golden brown. Meanwhile, tip the rest of the pizza sauce into a saucepan and heat through gently.

Serve the panzerotti with hot pizza sauce drizzled on top, garnished with a scattering of basil leaves.

Variations

For spicy beef panzerotti, omit the ham and mushrooms. Brown 200 g extra lean minced beef with 1 chopped green pepper and 1 sliced shallot, adding a pinch of crushed chillies and a chopped garlic clove. Cool before filling the panzerotti. The **ProPoints** values per serving will be 10.

 For vegetarian panzerotti, cook 1 sliced red or yellow pepper with the mushrooms, omit the ham from the filling ingredients and use vegetarian hard Italian cheese instead of the Parmesan. The **ProPoints** values per serving will be 8.

QUICK *Pineapple* Stir-fried Pork

6 ProPoints value

ProPoints values per serving
ProPoints values per recipe 23

GF

LC

Serves 4
Takes 20 minutes

1 teaspoon Chinese five spice
    powder
400 g lean stir-fry pork strips
200 g canned pineapple chunks in
    natural juice, drained and 20 ml
    juice reserved
1 tablespoon cornflour
3 tablespoons cider vinegar
2 tablespoons gluten free soy sauce
2 tablespoons tomato ketchup
    (ensure gluten free)
1 tablespoon soft light brown sugar
calorie controlled cooking spray
1 onion, sliced
3 mixed peppers, sliced
1 red chilli, sliced
2 garlic cloves, sliced
2 cm fresh root ginger, shredded
200 g pak choi, chopped roughly
salt and freshly ground black
    pepper

A classic sweet and sour stir-fry that is delicious served with noodles — a 50 g dried 'nest' per person will add 5 **ProPoints** values.

Sprinkle the Chinese five spice powder over the pork, season and mix well. Set aside.

Pour the reserved pineapple juice into a jug. Whisk in the cornflour, followed by the cider vinegar, soy sauce, tomato ketchup and sugar. Add 250 ml cold water and set aside.

Spray a wok or non-stick frying pan with the cooking spray and stir-fry the pork for 3 minutes over a high heat, until just cooked through. Remove to a plate.

Stir-fry the onion and peppers for 3–4 minutes before adding the chilli, garlic, ginger and pak choi. Cook for 2 minutes, stirring.

Return the pork to the wok or pan, tip in the pineapple chunks, give the sauce a stir and pour it in. Cook for 2 minutes, stirring as the sauce thickens to make sure that everything is well coated and combined. Serve immediately.

 Variation

Vegetarians can replace the pork with the same weight of Quorn Chicken Style Pieces. The **ProPoints** values per serving will be 4.

Mushroom FRIED Rice with *Omelette* Strips

 8 *ProPoints* values per serving
ProPoints values per recipe 30

 Serves 4
Takes 25 minutes

 GF

 HC

V

calorie controlled cooking spray
3 eggs, beaten
1 red chilli, chopped finely
3 tablespoons chopped fresh
    coriander
a bunch of spring onions, sliced
2 garlic cloves, crushed
2 cm fresh root ginger, shredded
250 g mushrooms, sliced
175 g frozen peas
500 g cold cooked brown rice
salt and freshly ground black
    pepper

Serve with a heap of lightly cooked broccoli and a drizzle of soy sauce, for no additional *ProPoints* values.

Spray a non-stick frying pan with the cooking spray. Beat the eggs, season and stir in the chilli and coriander. Pour into the pan and cook gently for 2–3 minutes until almost set. Slide out on to a plate and place the frying pan upside down over the omelette. Using an oven glove to hold the pan in place, flip the pan and plate over and cook the other side of the omelette for just 1 minute.

Slide the cooked omelette back out on to the plate and leave to cool slightly before slicing into strips.

Meanwhile, spray a wok or large non-stick frying pan with the cooking spray.

Fry the spring onions, garlic and ginger for 2 minutes before adding the mushrooms. Cook for 3 minutes, adding a splash of water at the start to help to cook the mushrooms.

Add the frozen peas to the pan and cook for 1 minute, then mix in the cooked rice.

Stir-fry for 3–4 minutes until the rice is piping hot. Mix in the omelette strips just before serving.

Cook's tip Fried rice is best made with cold cooked rice, in order to keep the rice grains separate. You can cook the rice a day ahead: you'll need 200 g dried brown rice – simply cook according to the packet instructions, drain and rinse in cold water. Cool before storing, covered, in the fridge.

Creamy *Thai* VEGETABLE Curry

 3 *ProPoints* values per serving
ProPoints values per recipe 13

 GF Serves 4
Preparation time 15 minutes
 V Cooking time 20 minutes

calorie controlled cooking spray
3 shallots, chopped roughly
350 g butternut squash, peeled and cubed
2 tablespoons red or green Thai curry paste (ensure gluten free)
200 ml light coconut milk
400 ml gluten free vegetable stock
100 g fine green beans, halved
75 g pineapple, chopped roughly
150 g cherry tomatoes, halved
salt and freshly ground black pepper

To serve
1 lime, quartered
chopped fresh coriander

The addition of pineapple to this vegetable curry really takes it to another dimension. To soak up the curry sauce, serve with 50 g dried brown rice per person, cooked according to the packet instructions, for an additional 5 *ProPoints* values per serving.

Spray a lidded saucepan with the cooking spray and cook the shallots for 2–3 minutes until softened.

Add the butternut squash and the Thai curry paste. Season and cook for 1 minute, stirring.

Pour the coconut milk and the stock into the pan, bring to the boil and then simmer, covered, for 10 minutes.

Stir the beans into the curry and cook, uncovered, for 7 minutes, or until the squash and beans are tender.

Add the pineapple and tomatoes to the curry and heat through for 1–2 minutes.

Ladle the curry into warmed bowls to serve, with a lime wedge to squeeze into the curry, and top with a scattering of fresh coriander.

Variation
You can turn this into a seafood Thai curry by adding 200 g cooked peeled king prawns with the pineapple and tomatoes. The *ProPoints* values per serving will be 4.

HOME at 7 Dinner by 8

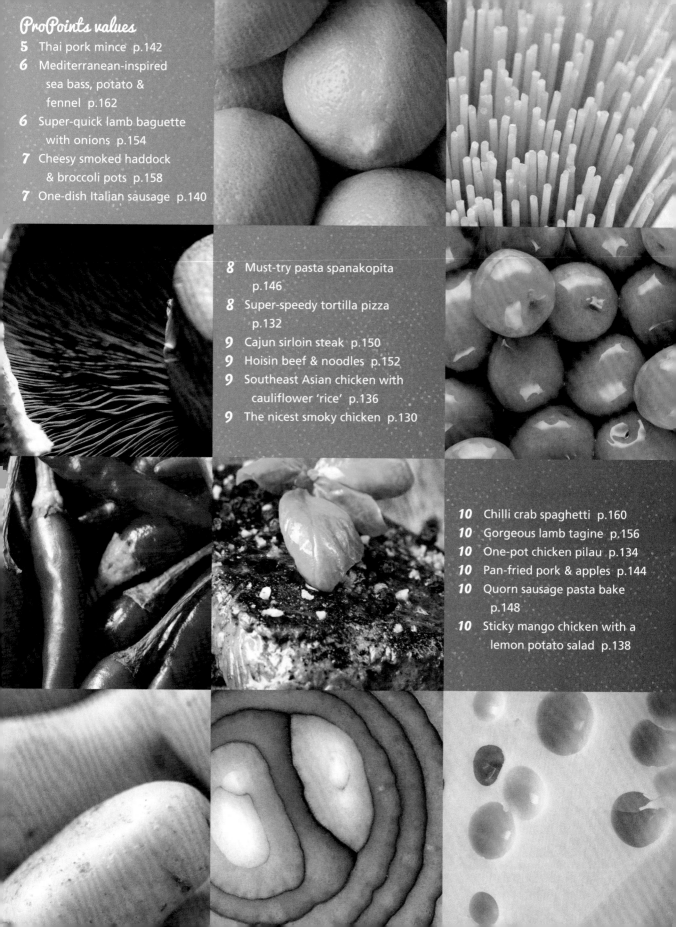

The NICEST *Smoky* Chicken

ProPoints values per serving **9**

ProPoints values per recipe 35

 Serves 4
Preparation time 20 minutes

 Cooking time 35–40 minutes

 800 g potatoes, cut into wedges

1¼ teaspoons smoked paprika

2 garlic cloves, crushed

1 tablespoon chopped fresh thyme, plus a few sprigs

calorie controlled cooking spray

1 large onion, cut into wedges

3 mixed peppers, cut into wedges

4 x 150 g skinless chicken breast fillets

2 oranges, 1 sliced and 1 cut into wedges

16 pimento-stuffed green olives

salt and freshly ground black pepper

This is a great all-in-one dish, with peppers, olives and oranges adding a vibrant Spanish flavour.

Preheat the oven to Gas Mark 7/220°C/fan oven 200°C and place a large roasting tray on the top shelf to preheat.

Add the potatoes to a pan of boiling water and bring back to the boil. Cook, covered, for 5 minutes.

Drain the potato wedges and shake gently to roughen up the edges. Sprinkle with 1 teaspoon smoked paprika, the garlic and chopped thyme, and mix gently to coat evenly.

Spray the hot tray with the cooking spray and tip the potato wedges on to the tray. Tuck in the onion and peppers, season and spray with extra cooking spray. Cook for 15 minutes.

Meanwhile, cut each chicken breast almost in half horizontally. Tuck a couple of orange slices and a sprig of thyme into each one. Dust with the remaining paprika and season lightly. Pop in the fridge, covered, until ready to cook.

When the 15 minutes are up, add the chicken breasts, orange wedges and olives to the oven tray. Cook for 15 minutes, or until the chicken is cooked through and the vegetables are starting to caramelise.

Super-speedy TORTILLA Pizza

 8 *ProPoints* **values per serving**
ProPoints **values per recipe 16**

HC

Serves 2
Takes 10 minutes

2 Weight Watchers tortillas, or
   similar
2 tablespoons tomato purée
100 g cooked skinless, boneless
   chicken breast, chopped
60 g sweetcorn
8 cherry tomatoes, quartered
a handful of fresh basil leaves
50 g half fat mature cheese, grated
salt and freshly ground black
   pepper

These no-fuss tortilla pizzas deliver all the flavour you'd expect, but are far lower in *ProPoints* values than a regular pizza, as well as being ready to eat in next to no time. Serve with a big mixed salad.

Preheat the grill.

Place the tortillas on a large baking tray and spread thinly with the tomato purée, all the way out to the edges.

Scatter the chicken, sweetcorn and tomatoes over each tortilla pizza, followed by the basil leaves and cheese. Season lightly.

Grill for 3–5 minutes (depending on how hot your grill gets), until the cheese is melted and bubbling and the tortilla is crisping up around the edges.

Cut into slices and serve immediately.

Variations

For a Hawaiian-style pizza, replace the chicken and sweetcorn with 2 x 35g premium ham slices, chopped, and 2 rings canned pineapple in juice, drained and chopped. The *ProPoints* values per serving will be 6.

V For a veggie version, fry ½ sliced pepper, 4 sliced spring onions and 75g sliced mushrooms in calorie controlled cooking spray before adding to the pizzas in place of the cooked chicken. The *ProPoints* values per serving will be 5.

One-pot CHICKEN *Pilau*

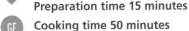

ProPoints values per serving
ProPoints values per recipe 41

Serves 4
Preparation time 15 minutes

Cooking time 50 minutes

calorie controlled cooking spray
1 onion, chopped roughly
2 courgettes, chopped roughly
1 red pepper, chopped roughly
2 teaspoons ground cumin
2 teaspoons ground coriander
½ teaspoon ground turmeric
grated zest and juice of 1 lemon
2 bay leaves
6 whole cloves
175 g dried brown rice
½ x 400 g can chickpeas, rinsed and
   drained
450 ml gluten free chicken stock
4 x 150 g skinless chicken breast
   fillets, slashed
salt and freshly ground black
   pepper

To serve
4 tablespoons 0% fat natural Greek
   yogurt
3 tablespoons chopped fresh
   coriander

A fantastic one-pot meal that needs no additional accompaniments, so there is very little washing up!

Preheat the oven to Gas Mark 4/180°C/fan oven 160°C.

Spray a lidded ovenproof casserole with the cooking spray and fry the onion for 3 minutes. Add the courgettes and pepper and cook for a further 2–3 minutes.

Meanwhile, combine the ground cumin, coriander, turmeric and lemon zest, and season. Reserve half the spice mixture for the chicken and add the rest to the casserole along with the bay leaves, cloves and rice. Cook for 1 minute, stirring.

Tip the chickpeas into the casserole and add half of the lemon juice and the stock. Bring to the boil, stir and cover. Bake in the oven for 20 minutes.

While the rice is cooking, rub the reserved spice mixture into the chicken breasts and drizzle with the rest of the lemon juice. Keep in the fridge, covered, until ready to use.

When the 20 minutes are up, pop the spiced chicken breasts on top of the rice, cover the casserole again and put it back in the oven for a further 20–30 minutes.

Remove the cloves and bay leaves from the rice (they tend to rise to the top during cooking) and serve the chicken pilau with the yogurt and coriander.

Cook's tip The leftover chickpeas can be added to a salad or used in a curry.

Southeast Asian *Chicken* with *Cauliflower* 'RICE'

9 *ProPoints* values per serving
ProPoints values per recipe 34

Serves 4
Preparation time 20 minutes +
marinating

Cooking time 45 minutes

4 x 200 g skinless chicken legs,
slashed
4 garlic cloves, sliced
100 ml gluten free dark soy sauce
100 ml cider vinegar
4 bay leaves
calorie controlled cooking spray
2 onions, sliced thickly
2 red peppers, sliced thickly
600 g cauliflower florets
salt and freshly ground black
pepper

To garnish
2 tablespoons chopped fresh flat
leaf parsley
1 red chilli, sliced

This chicken dish is a traditional Filipino recipe. Put the chicken in the marinade the night before (or in the morning), then it's ready to cook when you get in from work. The vinegar and garlic used in the marinade mellow as the chicken braises, and the resulting delicious sauce is soaked up by the zero *ProPoints* values cauliflower 'rice'.

Ahead of time, place the slashed chicken legs in a non-reactive lidded container or plastic food bag. Mix the garlic with the soy sauce, vinegar, 2 bay leaves and a generous grinding of black pepper. Pour over the chicken and turn to coat. Seal the container and marinate in the fridge for 4 hours or overnight.

When ready to cook, shake the marinade off the chicken legs (reserve the marinade), pat dry on kitchen paper and then brown in a preheated non-stick frying pan for 2–3 minutes each side.

Meanwhile, spray a flameproof casserole with calorie controlled cooking spray and fry the onions and peppers for about 4 minutes. Transfer the chicken legs to the casserole.

Pour the marinade into the frying pan to deglaze the pan, then tip this into the casserole; the sauce won't cover the meat but this doesn't matter. Cover the casserole and simmer gently for 45 minutes until the chicken is tender. The sauce will have a thin consistency.

Meanwhile, place the cauliflower florets in a steamer, season and tuck in the remaining bay leaves. Add boiling water to the base of the steamer, cover and cook for 12 minutes, or until the cauliflower is tender when pierced with a knife. Remove the cauliflower from the steamer and mash with a potato masher until it looks rather like rice.

Divide the cauliflower 'rice' between 4 bowls. Add a chicken leg to each bowl and spoon over the sauce. Garnish with parsley and chilli and serve.

Sticky Mango Chicken with a Lemon POTATO Salad

 ProPoints values per serving
ProPoints values per recipe 39

 Serves 4
Takes 25 minutes

 calorie controlled cooking spray

 4 x 150 g skinless chicken breast fillets

75 g mango chutney

2 tablespoons tomato ketchup (ensure gluten free)

1 garlic clove, crushed

2 cm fresh root ginger, grated

½ red chilli, chopped finely

grated zest and juice of ½ lemon

salt and freshly ground black pepper

For the potato salad

700 g new potatoes, cubed

grated zest and juice of ½ lemon

1 tablespoon extra virgin olive oil

3 tablespoons chopped fresh parsley

Mango chutney forms the basis of the spicy sticky glaze for the chicken here. Serve with some green beans alongside the warm potato salad for a quick and tasty dinner.

Preheat the grill, line a tray with foil and spray with the cooking spray.

Boil the potatoes for 15–20 minutes, or until tender.

While the potatoes are cooking, slash the chicken breasts and place on the foil-lined tray.

Mix together the mango chutney, tomato ketchup, garlic, ginger, chilli, lemon zest and juice, and season. Brush over the chicken breasts.

Grill the chicken breasts for 15 minutes, brushing with the glaze as they cook.

When the potatoes are cooked, drain them and stir in the lemon zest and juice, olive oil and parsley, and season.

Slice up the sticky mango chicken breasts and serve with the warm potato salad.

One-dish ITALIAN *Sausage*

 Serves 4
Preparation time 15 minutes
 Cooking time 40 minutes

800 g unpeeled potatoes, cut into
    wedges
calorie controlled cooking spray
8 Weight Watchers sausages, or
    similar, snipped into chunks
2 red onions, cut into wedges
1 red pepper, chopped roughly
1 yellow pepper, chopped roughly
3 garlic cloves, crushed
a pinch of dried chilli flakes
1 teaspoon fennel seeds
½ teaspoon dried rosemary
250 g cherry tomatoes, halved
salt and freshly ground black
    pepper

The punchy flavours of fennel seeds, chilli and garlic give this sausage and pepper traybake a southern Italian twist. Serve with lightly cooked broccoli.

Preheat the oven to Gas Mark 7/220°C/fan oven 200°C and place a large roasting tray on the top shelf to preheat.

Add the potato wedges to a large pan of boiling water, cover and cook for 10 minutes. Drain the wedges and shake them gently in the pan to slightly roughen the edges.

Spray the hot tray with the cooking spray, tip in the potato wedges, season lightly and spray with extra cooking spray. Cook for 10 minutes on the top shelf.

Meanwhile, combine the sausage chunks, onions, peppers, garlic, chilli flakes, fennel seeds and rosemary in a mixing bowl.

Add the sausage mixture to the roasting tray and spray with cooking spray. Cook for 20 minutes, stirring halfway through.

Add the cherry tomatoes to the roasting tray and cook for a final 10 minutes.

Divide between warmed plates to serve.

 Variation

For a veggie alternative, use 8 Quorn sausages in this recipe instead, for 8 *ProPoints* values per serving.

Cook's tip Fennel seeds have an aromatic sweet and slightly aniseedy flavour. They look very similar to cumin seeds but are greener in colour, and are frequently used in both Italian and Indian cooking.

Thai Pork Mince

 5 ProPoints *ProPoints* values per serving
ProPoints values per recipe 20

 Serves 4
Preparation time 10 minutes
 Cooking time 20 minutes

 GF calorie controlled cooking spray
500 g extra lean pork mince
LC 1 red chilli, de-seeded and chopped finely
3 garlic cloves, crushed
1 lemongrass stalk, chopped finely
1 red pepper, chopped
150 g mushrooms, quartered
1 tablespoon Thai fish sauce (ensure gluten free)
300 ml gluten free chicken stock
150 g sugar snap peas, sliced
juice of ½ lime
150 g beansprouts, rinsed
freshly ground black pepper
chopped fresh coriander, to garnish
lime wedges, to serve

Mince is so versatile, with an ability to take on all kinds of flavours. This Thai-inspired dish is really nice if you bulk it out with a 30 g portion of dried brown rice per person, cooked according to the packet instructions, for an extra 3 **ProPoints** values per serving.

Spray a flameproof casserole or large non-stick saucepan with the cooking spray and brown the mince over a high heat for 5 minutes, stirring to break it up.

Add the chilli, garlic, lemongrass, red pepper and mushrooms and cook for 2 minutes.

Add the fish sauce and stock, along with some black pepper, and bring to the boil. Cover and simmer the mince mixture for 15 minutes.

Mix in the sugar snap peas and cook for 5 minutes.

Stir in the lime juice and beansprouts then ladle the Thai pork mince into bowls. Garnish with coriander and serve with lime wedges.

 Variation

Try using Quorn mince in place of the pork mince (no need to brown it) and vegetable stock, with light soy sauce to replace the Thai fish sauce. The **ProPoints** values per serving will be 3.

Cook's tip You can use freeze-dried lemongrass in place of fresh if you prefer; simply re-hydrate 1 teaspoon of dried chopped lemongrass in a little boiling water for 5 minutes before use.

Pan-fried *Pork* & APPLES

 Serves 2
Takes 25–30 minutes

220 g potatoes, peeled and
  chopped
calorie controlled cooking spray
2 x 150 g pork steaks, trimmed of
  all fat
1 onion, sliced
1 teaspoon low fat spread
2 tablespoons redcurrant jelly
2 apples, cored and cut into wedges
1 tablespoon balsamic vinegar
100 ml gluten free chicken stock
a pinch of dried thyme
4 tablespoons skimmed milk
salt and freshly ground black
  pepper

A lovely autumnal dish that is great served with steamed broccoli florets.

Add the potatoes to a pan of boiling water and cook for 15–20 minutes until tender.

Meanwhile, spray a non-stick frying pan with the cooking spray and season the pork steaks.

Fry the pork steaks for 2½–3 minutes each side, with the onion scattered around the pork in the frying pan. Remove the pork and onion to a plate and wipe out the frying pan with kitchen paper.

Melt the low fat spread and 1 tablespoon of the redcurrant jelly together over a medium heat. Add the apple wedges, increase the heat and fry for about 1½ minutes each side, until the apples are starting to caramelise.

Add the balsamic vinegar to the pan and allow to bubble briefly before pouring in the stock and adding the thyme and the rest of the redcurrant jelly. Bring the sauce to the boil and return the pork and onions to the pan. Heat the pork steaks through for 1 minute each side.

Drain the potatoes and return to the pan. Add the skimmed milk, season and mash until smooth.

Serve the pork, apples and sauce on warmed plates with the mash.

Variation

You can substitute 2 x 150 g skinless chicken breast fillets for the pork if you prefer, for 7 *ProPoints* values per serving. The chicken will need 5–6 minutes each side to cook through, so don't add the onion until you turn the chicken over.

Must-try PASTA
Spanakopita

8 *ProPoints* values per serving
ProPoints values per recipe 34

Serves 4
Takes 20 minutes

250 g dried wholewheat pasta
  e.g. fusilli
40 g walnut halves
100 g young leaf spinach
1 small garlic clove, crushed
2 tablespoons chopped fresh mint
grated zest and juice of ½ lemon
60 g light feta cheese, crumbled
salt and freshly ground black
  pepper

A pesto-like spinach sauce and feta cheese coat wholewheat pasta in this recipe, with the crunch of toasted walnuts adding extra texture. Serve with a Greek-style salad of roughly chopped tomatoes, cucumber and Cos lettuce, dressed with lemon juice and a little dried mint.

Preheat the oven to Gas Mark 5/190°C/fan oven 170°C.

Add the pasta to a large pan of boiling water and cook according to the packet instructions.

Meanwhile, toast the walnuts in the oven for 5 minutes, then chop quite finely.

Place the spinach, garlic, mint, lemon zest and juice in a food processor (or use a hand-held blender), and add 4 tablespoons of the pasta cooking water. Whizz to a pesto-like purée and season to taste.

Drain the pasta, reserving a little of the cooking water. Return the pasta to the pan and tip in the spinach sauce, the feta and the walnuts. Mix together, adding enough of the extra pasta cooking water to give a sauce that coats the pasta.

Serve straightaway in warmed bowls.

Quorn Sausage PASTA Bake

 ProPoints values per serving
ProPoints values per recipe 38

 Serves 4
Preparation time 10 minutes
 Cooking time 40 minutes

calorie controlled cooking spray
200 g dried spaghetti
6 Quorn sausages, sliced thickly
400 g can chopped tomatoes
½ teaspoon dried mixed herbs
¼ teaspoon smoked paprika
3 tablespoons tomato ketchup
500 ml vegetable stock
150 g frozen peas
50 g half fat mature vegetarian
   cheese, grated
salt and freshly ground black
   pepper

This dish takes just 10 minutes to put together when you get home, and can then be left to bake while you get on with something else. Serve with a mixed salad on the side.

Preheat the oven to Gas Mark 6/200°C/fan oven 180°C and place a baking tray on the centre shelf.

Spray a 23 cm square baking dish with the cooking spray.

Roughly break up the spaghetti into the dish and add the sausages.

Combine the chopped tomatoes, mixed herbs, smoked paprika, ketchup and stock. Season, pour over the spaghetti and mix well.

Cover the dish tightly with foil. Place the dish on the preheated tray and bake for 30–35 minutes, or until the spaghetti is almost tender.

Remove the foil, stir in the peas and then scatter the cheese on top. Bake uncovered for a final 5 minutes.

Divide between 4 warmed plates or bowls to serve.

Variation
If you want to use 6 Weight Watchers sausages, or similar, in this recipe instead of the Quorn sausages, this will be 9 *ProPoints* values per serving. Spray a non-stick frying pan with calorie controlled cooking spray and brown the sausages for a couple of minutes before cutting into slices.

Cajun SIRLOIN Steak

 9 *ProPoints* values per serving
ProPoints values per recipe 38

Serves 4
Preparation time 20 minutes
 Cooking time 20 minutes

800 g sweet potatoes, peeled and
    cut into chips
calorie controlled cooking spray
1 teaspoon ground cumin
1 teaspoon ground coriander
1 teaspoon paprika
¼ teaspoon dried oregano
a pinch of cayenne pepper
1 garlic clove, crushed
grated zest and juice of ½ lime
4 x 125 g lean sirloin steaks
salt and freshly ground black
    pepper
lime wedges, to serve

For the salsa
175 g pineapple, chopped
1 shallot, sliced finely
½ red chilli, chopped finely
1 tablespoon chopped fresh mint
grated zest and juice of ½ lime

The pineapple salsa adds a bit of oomph to the spicy steak and sweet potato chips. Serve with a mixed leaf salad.

Preheat the oven to Gas Mark 7/220°C/fan oven 200°C and place a roasting tray on the top shelf to preheat.

Add the sweet potato chips to a pan of boiling water. Bring back to the boil and cook for 3 minutes then drain.

Spray the hot tray with the cooking spray and tip the sweet potato chips on to the tray. Season lightly and spray with a little more cooking spray. Roast in the oven for 20 minutes, turning halfway through.

In a small bowl, combine the spices with the garlic, lime zest and juice. Rub on to the steaks then pop them in the fridge on a plate until ready to cook.

For the salsa, mix the pineapple, shallot, chilli, mint, lime zest and juice together in a bowl and set aside.

When the sweet potato chips are nearly ready, cook the sirloin steaks on a preheated griddle pan (or non-stick frying pan) for 2–3 minutes each side, or until cooked to your liking.

Serve the steaks and chips with the salsa and a lime wedge.

Variations

Replace the steaks with 4 x 150 g skinless chicken breast fillets for 9 *ProPoints* values per serving. These will need to be cooked for 6–7 minutes each side to make sure that they are cooked through.

If you love fish, swap the steak for 4 x 125 g tuna steaks for 9 *ProPoints* values per serving. Cook the tuna for 2–3 minutes each side.

Hoisin BEEF & Noodles

 Serves 4
Takes 20 minutes

175 g dried rice noodles

calorie controlled cooking spray

400 g lean beef stir-fry strips

2 carrots, peeled and cut into matchsticks

200 g (7 oz) sugar snap peas, halved

2 garlic cloves, sliced

2 cm fresh root ginger, shredded

1½ teaspoons Chinese five spice powder

3 tablespoons hoisin sauce

125 ml beef stock

4 spring onions, sliced

As with most stir-fries, it definitely pays to do all the vegetable prep upfront before you start to cook, as the pace soon gets fast and furious!

Prepare the rice noodles according to the packet instructions and set them aside.

Spray a wok or large non-stick frying pan with the cooking spray and place over a high heat.

Stir-fry the beef for 2 minutes until starting to change colour.

Add the carrots, sugar snaps, garlic and ginger and cook for a further 2 minutes.

Sprinkle in the five spice powder then add the hoisin sauce and the stock. Simmer for 2 minutes until the vegetables are just tender and the sauce has reduced slightly.

Mix in the spring onions then serve the hoisin beef with the noodles.

 Variation

If you use gluten free hoisin sauce and stock this dish becomes suitable for a gluten free diet.

SUPER-QUICK *Lamb* Baguette with Onions

 6 *ProPoints* values per serving
ProPoints values per recipe 26

 Serves 4
Takes 15 minutes

4 Weight Watchers petits pains,
   or similar
300 g lean lamb leg steak
calorie controlled cooking spray
1 red onion, sliced
1 tablespoon redcurrant jelly
1 tablespoon chopped fresh mint
½ teaspoon smooth mustard
a squeeze of lemon juice
50 g mixed leaf salad
salt and freshly ground black
   pepper

Perfect for a speedy yet satisfying light meal when you get in late after work or a session at the gym! Serve with a tomato salad on the side.

Preheat the oven to Gas Mark 6/200°C/fan oven 180°C then bake the petits pains according to the packet instructions.

Season the lamb steaks. Spray a hot non-stick frying pan with the cooking spray and add the lamb and red onion to the pan. Cook the lamb for 2½–3 minutes each side, stirring the onions around as they cook. Remove the lamb to a plate and rest for a few minutes.

Meanwhile, mix the redcurrant jelly, mint and mustard together, adding a squeeze of lemon juice.

Split the petits pains and spread with the redcurrant jelly mixture. Slice the lamb, then tuck it, the onions and salad leaves into each petit pain. Serve immediately and enjoy!

Gorgeous Lamb TAGINE

 10 ProPoints values per serving
ProPoints values per recipe 42

Serves 4
Preparation time 20 minutes
Cooking time 30 minutes

 Tagine only

 400 g lean lamb leg, cubed
calorie controlled cooking spray
2 onions, chopped roughly
4 carrots, peeled and chopped
    roughly
1 teaspoon ground ginger
1 teaspoon ground cumin
1 teaspoon ground cinnamon
grated zest and juice of ½ lemon
300 ml vegetable stock
a pinch of saffron
salt and freshly ground black
    pepper
50 g pomegranate seeds, to serve

For the couscous
grated zest and juice of ½ lemon
1 teaspoon ground cinnamon
200 g dried wholewheat couscous
25 g toasted flaked almonds
4 tablespoons chopped fresh flat
    leaf parsley

Saffron and spices imbue this tagine with the flavours of sunny Morocco.

Season the lamb and brown in a lidded flameproof casserole, sprayed with the cooking spray, cooking the meat for about 5 minutes over a high heat, stirring occasionally.

Add the onions to the casserole and cook for 2–3 minutes until starting to brown.

Next add the carrots and the spices and stir to combine before adding the lemon zest and juice, the stock and saffron. Season to taste, bring to the boil then cover the casserole and reduce the heat. Simmer gently for 30 minutes, or until the lamb and vegetables are tender.

About 10 minutes before the tagine is ready, prepare the couscous: bring 350 ml water to the boil in a lidded saucepan. Add the lemon zest and juice, cinnamon and a pinch of salt. Tip in the couscous, stir briefly then cover with the lid. Remove from the heat and leave to stand and swell for 5 minutes.

Stir the almonds and half the parsley into the couscous and fluff up with a fork.

Serve the tagine ladled over the couscous, scattered with the remaining parsley and the pomegranate seeds.

Cheesy Smoked Haddock & BROCCOLI Pots

7 *ProPoints* values per serving
ProPoints values per recipe 27

GF

LC

Serves 4
Preparation time 25 minutes
Cooking time 10 minutes

500 g smoked haddock
600 ml skimmed milk
300 g broccoli florets
2 tablespoons cornflour
75 g mature half fat cheese, grated
25 g packet reduced fat ready salted crisps (ensure gluten free)
salt and freshly ground black pepper

A really comforting supper dish of smoked haddock and broccoli bathed in cheese sauce with a crunchy crisp topping. Serve with 150 g new potatoes per person, for an additional 3 *ProPoints* values per serving.

Preheat the oven to Gas Mark 7/220°C/fan oven 200°C.

Place the smoked haddock in a non-stick pan and pour in the milk. Season with freshly ground black pepper, partially cover with a lid and bring to the boil. Reduce the heat and simmer for about 4 minutes, until the fish starts to flake.

Meanwhile, cook the broccoli in boiling water for 3–4 minutes until just tender. Drain well.

Remove the fish from the pan and break into large flakes. Strain the milk into a jug. Rinse out the pan.

Add the cornflour to the pan and gradually blend in the strained milk. Place on the heat and bring to the boil, stirring. Simmer the sauce for 3 minutes.

While the sauce is cooking, divide the broccoli and smoked haddock between 4 individual heatproof dishes (or use 1 large dish).

Remove the sauce from the heat, stir in two-thirds of the cheese and season to taste. Pour over the broccoli and smoked haddock. Crush the crisps and mix with the rest of the cheese, then scatter on top of each dish. Bake for 10 minutes until bubbling and golden brown.

Chilli *Crab* SPAGHETTI

 ProPoints values per serving
ProPoints values per recipe 20

 Serves 2
Takes 15 minutes

150 g dried wholewheat spaghetti
2 teaspoons extra virgin olive oil
2 garlic cloves, sliced
½ red chilli, chopped finely
100 ml vegetable or chicken stock
grated zest and juice of ½ lemon
170 g can white crabmeat, drained
50 g wild rocket
salt and freshly ground black
    pepper

A hearty bowlful of seafood spaghetti, packed with punchy flavours.

Add the spaghetti to a large pan of boiling water. Cook according to the packet instructions.

Meanwhile, place the olive oil, garlic and chilli together in a small pan and heat gently for about 2 minutes, or until the garlic just starts to turn golden.

Add the stock, lemon zest and juice to the chilli-garlic oil and boil for 2 minutes, or until slightly reduced.

Drain the cooked spaghetti and return to the pan. Pour in the lemony sauce and add the drained crabmeat and rocket. Mix together well and serve in warmed bowls.

Variation
If you don't fancy crab, try this recipe with 150 g cooked peeled prawns instead, for 10 **ProPoints** values per serving.

Cook's tip If you heat the garlic and chilli in the olive oil from cold, the garlic is less likely to burn quickly (although you still need to keep an eye on the pan), but will still infuse the olive oil with bags of flavour.

Mediterranean-inspired
Sea Bass, POTATO & Fennel

 ProPoints values per serving
ProPoints values per recipe 25

GF

Serves 4
Preparation time 15 minutes

HC

Cooking time 25 minutes

M

4 teaspoons extra virgin olive oil
600 g new potatoes, sliced
1 fennel bulb, sliced (fronds
   reserved for garnish)
1 onion, sliced
1 lemon, sliced
2 garlic cloves, sliced
a pinch of chilli flakes
6 plum tomatoes, quartered
4 x 80 g sea bass fillets, skin scored
salt and freshly ground black
   pepper

A Mediterranean-influenced meal, reminiscent of holiday sunshine even on a dull day.

Preheat the oven to Gas Mark 7/220°C/fan oven 200°C and place a large roasting tray on the top shelf to preheat.

Drizzle 3 teaspoons of the olive oil over the new potatoes, sliced fennel, onion, lemon, garlic and chilli flakes, and mix to coat evenly. Season to taste.

Tip the potato mixture on to the preheated tray and cook for 10 minutes.

Give the vegetables a stir and add the tomatoes to the tray. Cook for another 10 minutes.

Meanwhile, rub the remaining teaspoon of olive oil and some salt and black pepper into the skin side of the sea bass fillets. Add the fillets to a hot non-stick frying pan, skin side down, and press the fillets down to crisp the skin. Cook for 1½ minutes, or until starting to crisp up, then remove immediately so that they don't overcook.

Add the part-cooked sea bass fillets to the oven tray, skin side up, and cook everything for a further 5 minutes.

Scatter the fennel fronds over, just before serving.

> *Cook's tip* If you fancied eating this as part of a Filling & Healthy day approach, just remember to count the extra virgin olive oil either as part of your daily two teaspoons of healthy oil or out of your weekly allowance.

MAKE the MOST of 5

Quick PEA 'Guacamole'

 ProPoints value per serving
ProPoints values per recipe 5

 Serves 4
Takes 10 minutes

 200 g frozen peas

 1 garlic clove, sliced

2 tablespoons 0% fat natural Greek yogurt

2 ripe tomatoes, peeled, de-seeded and cubed

2 teaspoons finely chopped red onion or shallot

1 tablespoon chopped fresh coriander

a squeeze of lime juice

a shake of Tabasco sauce

salt and freshly ground black pepper

A sweet pea purée forms the basis of this dip in place of the usual avocado. Serve with zero **ProPoints** values vegetable crudités, such as carrots, peppers and radishes, or accompany with some home-made tortilla chips (see the Cook's tip below).

Add the frozen peas and garlic to a pan of boiling water. Bring back to the boil and cook for 3–4 minutes until tender.

Drain the peas and garlic, and rinse in cold water to stop them cooking any further. Shake dry then tip the peas and garlic into a food processor (or use a hand-held blender). Add the Greek yogurt and blend to a purée.

Stir in the tomatoes, onion and coriander, and add a squeeze of lime juice and a shake of Tabasco sauce. Season to taste then transfer to a serving bowl and chill until ready to serve.

Cook's tips To make quick and easy home-made tortilla chips, preheat the oven to Gas Mark 4/180°C/fan oven 160°C. Lightly spray 3 Weight Watchers tortillas, or similar, on both sides with calorie controlled cooking spray. Season and dust lightly with smoked paprika. Cut each tortilla into 4 strips, and then snip these into triangles with kitchen scissors. Spread out in a single layer on a large baking tray and bake in the oven for 6–8 minutes until golden brown and crisp. The *ProPoints* values per serving will be 3.

To peel fresh tomatoes, cut a shallow cross in the base of each one and place in a bowl. Cover the tomatoes with boiling water and leave to stand for about 1 minute. Drain, and the skin should slip off easily if the tomato is ripe. Quarter the tomatoes and scrape out the seeds, which would add too much liquid to the dip.

Thai *Butternut* SQUASH Soup

 ProPoints value per serving
ProPoints values per recipe 7

 Serves 6
Preparation time 15 minutes

 Cooking time 20 minutes

calorie controlled cooking spray
1 onion, chopped roughly
5 cm fresh root ginger, sliced
2 garlic cloves, crushed
1 red chilli, de-seeded and sliced
1 lemongrass stalk, sliced
900 g butternut squash, peeled,
    de-seeded and chopped roughly
900 ml gluten free vegetable stock
200 ml light coconut milk
grated zest and juice of ½ lime
salt and freshly ground black
    pepper
3 tablespoons chopped fresh
    coriander, to garnish

Butternut squash makes a beautiful velvety-textured soup, with classic Thai flavourings added here for a warming variation.

Spray a large lidded saucepan with the cooking spray and cook the onion for 2 minutes.

Meanwhile, place the ginger, garlic, chilli and lemongrass in a small food processor and whizz until finely chopped (or use a hand-held blender). Add to the saucepan and cook for 1 minute, stirring.

Add the butternut squash plus 5 tablespoons of the stock, cover the pan and cook for 5 minutes over a medium heat.

Pour the rest of the stock and the coconut milk into the pan and season. Bring to the boil and simmer, covered, for 15 minutes until the squash is soft.

Blend the soup with the lime zest and juice until smooth. Serve garnished with coriander.

Best-ever *Root Vegetable* CRISPS

 ProPoints values per serving
ProPoints values per recipe 10

Serves 4

Preparation time 20 minutes + drying

Cooking time 10 minutes

1 parsnip, peeled
1 carrot, peeled
1 small sweet potato, peeled
1 raw beetroot, peeled
3 teaspoons olive oil
¼ teaspoon ground cumin
salt and freshly ground black pepper

Root vegetable crisps are a gourmet choice with a high price tag, but here you will discover how to create a delicious home-made version that is low in *ProPoints* values.

Using a mandoline, a food processor slicing blade, a swivel peeler or even a kitchen knife and a steady hand, cut each vegetable into thin slices, keeping the batches separate.

In turn, very lightly sprinkle each batch of vegetables with salt and spread them out in a single layer on absorbent kitchen paper (the beetroot will need a double thickness). Place more kitchen paper on top and leave to stand for 15 minutes, pressing down to absorb any excess liquid from the vegetables. This makes sure that they will crisp up properly in the oven. Preheat the oven to Gas Mark 4/180°C/fan oven 160°C.

Combine the parsnip, carrot and sweet potato slices in a bowl with 2 teaspoons of the olive oil. Spread them out in a single layer on a large baking tray. Repeat with the beetroot and remaining teaspoon of olive oil, spreading out on another large baking tray.

Bake in the oven for 8–10 minutes until the vegetables are looking dry and starting to curl and colour at the edges. Remove from the oven and leave to cool and crisp up on the trays.

Tip all the crisps into a bowl and sprinkle with the ground cumin and a grinding of black pepper.

Cook's tip The vegetable crisps don't retain their crispness for more than a couple of hours if left to stand uncovered. Store in an airtight container if you're not going to eat them straightaway. However, it is possible to re-crisp them by baking for 3–4 minutes at Gas Mark 4/180°C/fan oven 160°C, spread out on a baking tray.

HOME-made *Popcorn*

 ProPoints values per serving
ProPoints values per recipe 12

 Serves 4
Takes 10 minutes

75 g popping corn
½ teaspoon flavourless oil e.g.
    groundnut or sunflower
½ teaspoon butter
salt

Home-made popcorn is a great low *ProPoints* values nibble. Below are some sweet and savoury flavour ideas.

Toss the popcorn in the oil, in a large microwaveable bowl. Cover the bowl with cling film and pierce once or twice.

Set the microwave on full power for 4 minutes, but stay nearby as the popcorn may not need all this time and can start to burn if overcooked. You may want to decant the popped corn after 3 minutes, re-cover the bowl and return the unpopped kernels to the microwave to carry on cooking.

Listen out for the popcorn as it pops; when the popping slows down to one pop every 5–10 seconds, remove the bowl from the microwave and peel off the cling film (watch out for steam escaping). Add the butter to the popcorn and stir as it melts. Sprinkle with salt and serve.

Variations: 3 *ProPoints* values per serving
Sweet popcorn: before serving, add 1 teaspoon caster sugar, vanilla sugar or cinnamon sugar; or drizzle with 2 teaspoons maple syrup and mix well; or add 1 teaspoon caster sugar and 10 g finely grated dark chocolate. **Savoury popcorn:** before serving, sprinkle in ¼ teaspoon ground cumin and a pinch of smoked paprika; or add 15 g finely grated vegetarian hard Italian cheese, 1 teaspoon fresh thyme leaves and ½ teaspoon finely grated lemon zest.

Cook's tip You can also prepare the popcorn on the hob. Heat the oil in a large lidded saucepan over a medium heat, until smoking hot. Tip in the popcorn and shake to coat. Clamp the lid on tightly and place back on the hob. As soon as you hear the popcorn start to pop, reduce the heat to low and shake the pan occasionally, until the popping slows down to one pop every 5–10 seconds. Remove from the heat, add the butter and salt and mix to coat.

Smoky

Cheese &
thyme

Butter

Maple

Chocolate

Cinnamon
sugar

Turkey STIR-FRY with a Kick

 ProPoints values per serving
ProPoints values per recipe 13

Serves 4
Takes 30 minutes

 500 g diced turkey breast
 calorie controlled cooking spray
4 shallots, sliced
4 cm fresh root ginger, shredded
3 garlic cloves, sliced
1 red chilli, sliced
200 g broccoli, broken into small florets
150 ml gluten free chicken stock
200 g pak choi, separated into leaves and stems, chopped roughly
200 g beansprouts, rinsed
juice of 1 lime
1½ tablespoons Thai fish sauce (ensure gluten free)
salt and freshly ground black pepper

A zingy, spicy stir-fry bursting with fresh flavours.

Season the turkey and spray a wok or large non-stick frying pan with the cooking spray. Stir-fry the turkey for 5 minutes over a high heat. Transfer to a plate.

Tip the shallots, ginger, garlic and chilli into the wok or frying pan and stir-fry for 2 minutes. Add the broccoli and 4 tablespoons of the stock, and steam-fry for 3 minutes, adding another 2 tablespoons of stock as the first addition evaporates.

Add the pak choi stems plus 2 tablespoons of stock to the wok or pan and cook for a further 2 minutes. Finally add the pak choi leaves, beansprouts, browned turkey plus the rest of the stock, the lime juice and fish sauce. Stir-fry for 2–3 minutes then serve immediately.

 Variation

Vegetarians can replace the diced turkey breast with the same weight of Quorn Chicken Style Pieces. Add them with the pak choi leaves and beansprouts as there is no need to par-cook the Quorn before adding it to the stir-fry. The **ProPoints** values per serving will be 4.

The BEST *Chicken* Kebabs

 ProPoints values per serving
ProPoints values per recipe 16

 Serves 4

Preparation time 20 minutes +
   marinating

 Cooking time 15 minutes

100 g fat-free natural yogurt
1 garlic clove, crushed
1 teaspoon ground cumin
½ teaspoon dried mint
grated zest and juice of 1 lemon
500 g cubed skinless chicken breast
1 red pepper, chopped roughly
1 green pepper, chopped roughly
1 red onion, chopped roughly
salt and freshly ground black
   pepper

To serve

150 g 0% fat natural Greek yogurt
1 small garlic clove, crushed
6 tomatoes, sliced
1 small red onion, sliced thinly
1 tablespoon chopped fresh mint

These fragrant kebabs are wonderful cooked on the barbecue if the weather permits. If you have **ProPoints** to spare, serve with a wholemeal pitta bread for an additional 4 **ProPoints** values per person.

Ahead of time, combine the yogurt with the garlic, cumin, mint, lemon zest and juice to make a marinade. Season, stir in the chicken then cover and marinate in the fridge for at least 2 hours, or overnight.

When ready to cook, preheat the grill. Thread the marinated chicken on to 8 skewers, along with the peppers and red onion.

Grill for 15 minutes, turning occasionally, until cooked through and charred at the edges.

Meanwhile, to make a quick relish mix the Greek yogurt and garlic, and season. Arrange the tomatoes on a serving platter, season and scatter with the red onion and mint.

Serve the kebabs with the tomato salad and garlicky yogurt relish.

Cook's tip When using wooden skewers, soak them first in cold water for about 30 minutes, to stop them from burning under the grill.

Simple *Beef* STEW

 4 *ProPoints* values per serving
ProPoints values per recipe 23

 Serves 6
 Preparation time 20 minutes
Cooking time 1½ hours

calorie controlled cooking spray
1 onion, chopped roughly
2 celery sticks, chopped roughly
4 carrots, chopped roughly
2 garlic cloves, crushed
1 tablespoon plain flour
1 teaspoon ground cinnamon
500 g cubed lean beef stewing steak
2 tablespoons tomato purée
3 tablespoons balsamic vinegar
125 ml red wine
400 ml beef stock
¼ teaspoon dried thyme
salt and freshly ground black
    pepper
fresh thyme leaves, to garnish
    (optional)

This richly flavoured stew is a doddle to put together, and there's not even any need to brown the meat. Serve with mashed carrot and swede, and a pile of lightly cooked vibrant green cabbage, for a zero *ProPoints* values side.

Preheat the oven to Gas Mark 2/150°C/fan oven 130°C.

Spray a lidded ovenproof casserole with the cooking spray and brown the onion, celery and carrots over a high heat for about 4 minutes. Add the garlic and cook for 1 minute.

Meanwhile, combine the flour and cinnamon, and season. Toss the beef in the spiced flour to coat. Tip the beef and any extra flour into the casserole along with the tomato purée and balsamic vinegar. Pour in the red wine and stock, and sprinkle in the thyme.

Bring the stew to the boil, cover with a lid and place in the oven to cook for 1½ hours until the meat and vegetables are tender.

Cook's tip This is an ideal recipe to cook in a slow cooker. Prepare the ingredients as above, but reduce the stock to 200 ml, as you don't need as much liquid for slow cooker stews. Cook on low for around 8 hours, or on high for 4–6 hours.

CLASSIC Seafood *Stew*

5 *ProPoints* values per serving
ProPoints values per recipe 21

GF
M
LC

Serves 4
Preparation time 20 minutes
Cooking time 20 minutes

1 tablespoon olive oil

1 onion, sliced thinly

3 garlic cloves, chopped

1 fennel bulb, sliced thinly and
   fronds reserved

a pinch of dried chilli flakes

1 red or orange pepper, sliced

1 yellow pepper, sliced

500 ml gluten free vegetable or
   chicken stock

400 g can chopped tomatoes

250 g new potatoes, sliced

grated zest of ½ orange

200 g firm skinless white fish fillet,
   cubed

350 g seafood selection, defrosted
   if frozen

salt and freshly ground black
   pepper

Garlic, chilli and fennel imbue this hearty fish stew with the classic flavours of the South of France.

Heat the olive oil in a large, flameproof, lidded casserole and cook the onion, garlic and fennel for 4 minutes, uncovered, over a medium heat, stirring occasionally.

Add the chilli flakes, peppers and 100 ml of the stock. Cover and cook for 5 minutes until the vegetables start to soften.

Tip the tomatoes into the casserole with the rest of the stock, the sliced potatoes and the orange zest. Season, bring to the boil and cook, covered, for 15 minutes, or until the potatoes are tender.

Stir the fish and seafood mix into the casserole and cook gently for 4–5 minutes until the fish is just starting to flake and the seafood is heated through.

Ladle into deep bowls and serve scattered with the fennel fronds.

Cook's tip Fennel adds a light aniseed-like flavour to this stew. You can use 1 sliced leek and 2 chopped celery sticks instead of the fennel, if you prefer.

Oriental Fish PARCELS

 3 *ProPoints* values per serving
ProPoints values per recipe 12

 Serves 4
Preparation time 15 minutes
 Cooking time 15 minutes

calorie controlled cooking spray
75 g young leaf spinach
1 red pepper, sliced
4 x 150 g pieces thick skinless white
    fish fillet
125 g shiitake mushrooms, sliced
150 g sugar snap peas, halved
2 spring onions, sliced
2.5 cm fresh root ginger, shredded
3 tablespoons gluten free dark
    soy sauce
1 tablespoon rice vinegar

These fish parcels can be prepared a couple of hours ahead of time, ready to pop in the oven when you want to eat. Serve with 50 g nutty-tasting dried brown rice per person, cooked according to the packet instructions, for an extra 5 *ProPoints* values per serving.

Preheat the oven to Gas Mark 6/200°C/fan oven 180°C.

Prepare 4 sheets of foil, measuring about 30 x 50 cm, and spray each one with the cooking spray. Lay all 4 out on the work surface.

Divide the spinach and red pepper between the sheets of foil, piling them up in the centre of each one. Sit a piece of fish on top.

Scatter the mushrooms, sugar snaps and spring onions over the fish. Combine the ginger, soy sauce and rice vinegar in a small bowl and drizzle 1 tablespoon over each piece of fish.

Bring the foil up around the fish and vegetables, leaving plenty of room for air to circulate and scrunch the edges together tightly to seal the parcels. Place on a baking tray.

Bake for 12–15 minutes, depending on the thickness of the fish fillets. Serve immediately.

Variation

If you're not on a Filling & Healthy day, you can add some noodles to these parcels. Precook 4 x 40 g 'nests' of dried wholewheat egg noodles or soba noodles following the instructions on the packet. Drain and rinse in cold water. Use these as the first layer in assembling the parcels. The *ProPoints* values per serving will be 7.

Cook's tip If you don't have any rice vinegar, use 1 tablespoon lime juice or lemon juice instead.

Seared COD with CHILLI Broccoli

4 *ProPoints* values per serving
ProPoints values per recipe 8

Serves 2
Takes 15–20 minutes

2 teaspoons extra virgin olive oil
2 x 150 g skinless cod loin fillets
1 garlic clove, sliced
½ red chilli, chopped
2 tablespoons shredded fresh basil
grated zest and juice of ½ lemon
175 g cherry tomatoes, quartered
200 g tenderstem broccoli or
    broccoli florets
salt and freshly ground black
    pepper

A garlicky, spicy fresh tomato sauce gives this fish dish an Italian-style twist.

Rub ½ teaspoon of the olive oil into the cod fillets and season lightly. Add the cod fillets to a preheated non-stick frying pan and cook for 4–5 minutes each side, depending on the thickness of the fish. The cod should have a golden brown exterior, and the flakes should just start to pull apart.

Meanwhile, put the rest of the olive oil in a small pan with the garlic and chilli. Heat until the garlic is just starting to turn golden then add the basil, lemon zest, tomatoes and 1 tablespoon of water. Season and cook for 4–5 minutes until the tomatoes are starting to soften and break down.

Boil the broccoli for 3–4 minutes until tender, then drain thoroughly and divide between 2 warmed plates.

Add the lemon juice to the tomato sauce and spoon over the broccoli. Lay the cod on top and serve immediately.

> *Cook's tip* If you fancied eating this as part of a Filling & Healthy day approach, just remember to count the extra virgin olive oil either as part of your daily two teaspoons of healthy oil or out of your weekly allowance.

Butternut SQUASH & Goat's Cheese Frittata

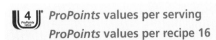 *ProPoints* values per serving
ProPoints values per recipe 16

GF
M
LC
V

Serves 4
Preparation time 15 minutes
Cooking time 55 minutes

500 g (1 lb 2 oz) butternut squash,
   cubed
2 red onions, cut into wedges
1 garlic clove, crushed
calorie controlled cooking spray
100 g goat's cheese, crumbled
3 eggs
1 egg white
2 tablespoons Weight Watchers
   crème fraîche, or similar
1 tablespoon chopped fresh thyme
salt and freshly ground black
   pepper

Goat's cheese combines beautifully with roasted butternut squash, red onion and thyme in this oven-baked frittata. Serve with a leafy green salad.

Preheat the oven to Gas Mark 6/200°C/fan oven 180°C. Toss the squash, red onion wedges and garlic together in a 20 cm non-stick pie dish. Season, spray with the cooking spray and roast for 30 minutes until tender, stirring occasionally.

Remove the pie dish from the oven, reducing the temperature to Gas Mark 3/160°C/fan oven 140°C, and nestle the goat's cheese in among the vegetables.

Whisk together the whole eggs, egg white, crème fraîche and thyme, and season. Pour all over the roasted vegetables and goat's cheese. Return to the cooler oven and bake for 25 minutes, or until set. Pop under a hot grill for 2–3 minutes to brown the cheese.

Leave to stand for 5 minutes before slicing into wedges to serve.

Broccoli & BLUE CHEESE *Gratin*

5 ProPoints values per serving
ProPoints values per recipe 9

Serves 2
Takes 15 minutes

1 tablespoon cornflour
300 ml skimmed milk
¼ gluten free vegetable stock cube, crumbled
400 g broccoli florets
40 g strong blue cheese, crumbled, e.g. vegetarian Stilton
10 cherry tomatoes, halved
1 spring onion, sliced
1 teaspoon chopped fresh parsley
salt and freshly ground black pepper

If you're craving something deeply savoury and cheesy but don't have many *ProPoints* values to spare, this recipe will come to your rescue.

Preheat the grill.

Place the cornflour in a non-stick saucepan and gradually whisk in the milk. Add the crumbled stock cube and bring to the boil, stirring until the sauce thickens. Simmer for 5 minutes.

Meanwhile, cook the broccoli florets in boiling water for 3–4 minutes until just tender. Drain well and transfer to a heatproof dish.

Stir the blue cheese into the sauce and adjust the seasoning to taste. Pour the cheese sauce over the broccoli and scatter the cherry tomatoes and spring onion on top.

Grill for 4–5 minutes until the sauce is bubbling and flecked with golden brown patches. Garnish with chopped parsley.

Variations

You can replace the broccoli florets with cauliflower if you prefer, or use a combination of the two.

For a more traditional cauliflower (or broccoli) cheese, replace the blue cheese with 40 g grated mature half fat cheese, plus a dab of smooth mustard to bring out the flavour in the sauce. The *ProPoints* values per serving will be 4.

Desserts & Bakes

Mocha WALNUT *Brownies*

 3 *ProPoints* **values per brownie**
ProPoints **values per recipe 51**

 * Makes 16 brownies
Preparation time 10 minutes

 HC **Cooking time 20 minutes**

V 25 g chopped walnuts
175 g self-raising flour
25 g cocoa powder
a pinch of salt
125 g light brown soft sugar
2 tablespoons instant coffee
granules
100 g fat-free natural yogurt
1 egg, beaten
150 ml cold water
75 g low fat spread, melted

Coffee and walnuts add extra flavour to these tempting brownies. Enjoy them over a cup of coffee with friends.

Preheat the oven to Gas Mark 4/180°C/fan oven 160°C. Toast the walnuts on a baking tray for 5 minutes. Line a 20 cm square cake tin with non-stick baking parchment.

Sift the flour, cocoa and salt into a mixing bowl. Stir in the sugar and chopped walnuts.

Dissolve the coffee in 1 tablespoon of boiling water. Whisk together the yogurt, egg and cold water, then add the coffee. Pour the mixture into the bowl of dry ingredients, along with the melted low fat spread. Stir to mix well.

Pour the brownie batter into the prepared tin and bake for 20 minutes on the centre shelf until the brownies are set and the top looks slightly cracked.

Cool the brownies in the tin before cutting into 16 squares. Store in an airtight tin for up to 2 days, or wrap well and freeze.

Variation
If you don't like the flavour of coffee, omit both the coffee and walnuts from the recipe and replace with 1 teaspoon vanilla extract in the brownie mixture, plus 25 g white chocolate chips. The *ProPoints* values per serving will be 3.

Lemon & LIME *Crunch* Cake

3 *ProPoints* values per slice
ProPoints values per recipe 42

Makes 12 slices
Preparation time 10 minutes
Cooking time 35–40 minutes

175 g self-raising flour
½ teaspoon baking powder
a pinch of salt
60 g low fat spread
100 g caster sugar
1 egg, beaten
grated zest and juice of 1 lemon
grated zest and juice of 1 lime
150 g fat-free natural yogurt
40 g demerara sugar

Lemon drizzle cake is one of the nation's favourites. This low *ProPoints* value version also adds lime zest and juice.

Preheat the oven to Gas Mark 4/180°C/fan oven 160°C. Line a 900 g loaf tin with non-stick baking parchment.

Sift the flour, baking powder and salt into a small bowl.

In a mixing bowl, cream the low fat spread and caster sugar together for about 3 minutes using an electric mixer.

Beat in the egg and two-thirds of the lemon and lime zests. Add half of the flour to the mixing bowl and mix briefly, followed by half of the yogurt and mix again. Repeat with the rest of the flour mixture and yogurt. Don't over-mix or the sponge will be rubbery. The mixture will be quite stiff compared to a standard sponge cake batter.

Spoon the cake mixture into the prepared loaf tin and spread out evenly. Bake on the centre shelf for 35–40 minutes. A skewer pushed into the centre of the cake should come out clean when it is cooked. Remove the cake from the oven.

Quickly mix together the rest of the citrus zest with the lemon and lime juice and the demerara sugar. Use a skewer or fork to make little holes all over the cake, spoon the citrus drizzle on top and leave to soak in. Cool the cake in the loaf tin.

Store in an airtight tin for up to 3 days.

> *Cook's tip* To get more juice out of citrus fruit, warm them for 15–30 seconds in the microwave before halving and squeezing. Alternatively, simply roll the whole fruit on the work surface, pressing down firmly as you do so, to release more juice.

Banana & PISTACHIO Cupcakes

4 *ProPoints* values per cupcake
ProPoints values per recipe 51

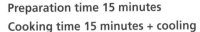

Makes 12
Preparation time 15 minutes
Cooking time 15 minutes + cooling

calorie controlled cooking spray
100 g light brown soft sugar
80 g low fat soft spread
2 eggs
½ tablespoon vanilla extract
4 ripe medium bananas, about
   400 g before peeling, mashed
225 g self-raising flour
a pinch of salt
40 g pistachio kernels, chopped

Green pistachios stud these little banana-flavoured cupcakes. Make sure that you buy unsalted shelled pistachio kernels from the baking aisle, rather than salted pistachios in the shell.

Preheat the oven to Gas Mark 4/180°C/fan oven 160°C. Spray a 12-hole non-stick muffin tray with the cooking spray.

Beat the sugar and low fat spread together in a mixing bowl for 2 minutes, using an electric mixer. Add the eggs, one at a time, whisking again after each one.

Add the vanilla and stir in the mashed bananas. Sift the flour and salt into the banana mixture then sprinkle in about three-quarters of the chopped pistachios. Stir to combine.

Spoon the mixture into the prepared muffin tray, dividing it evenly between the 12 holes. Sprinkle with the reserved pistachios. Bake the cupcakes on the centre shelf for 15 minutes until risen, golden brown and firm and springy to the touch.

Cool in the tin for 5 minutes then turn out on to a wire rack to finish cooling. Store in an airtight container for up to 2 days, or wrap well and freeze.

Cook's tip This recipe is a great way to use up over-ripe bananas. When your bananas turn too brown and speckly for your liking, pop them, whole, in the freezer until you are ready to use them in baking. Defrost at room temperature, or zap in the microwave. When you squeeze the banana out of its skin, the texture is perfect for mashing.

Ginger OAT Cookies

 2 *ProPoints* values per cookie
ProPoints values per recipe 33

 Makes 16
Preparation time 10 minutes
 Cooking time 15 minutes

125 g self-raising flour
1½ teaspoons ground ginger
60 g demerara sugar
40 g porridge oats
100 g low fat spread

These crunchy cookies are just the thing to have with a cup of tea when you fancy a sweet snack.

Preheat the oven to Gas Mark 4/180°C/fan oven 160°C. Line a large baking tray with non-stick baking parchment.

Sift the flour and ginger into a mixing bowl then stir in the sugar and porridge oats.

Add the low fat spread and use a wooden spoon to bring the ingredients together in a slightly sticky ball of dough.

Use a tablespoon measure to create 16 balls of dough and space them out on the lined tray. Press down to flatten them into cookies.

Bake on the centre shelf for 12–15 minutes until the cookies are a light golden brown, turning the tray around halfway through cooking so that they colour evenly.

Cool the cookies on the tray until set, then transfer to a wire rack to finish cooling. Store in an airtight container for up to a week.

Tropical MERINGUE Crush

2 *ProPoints* values per serving
ProPoints values per recipe 9

 Serves 4
Takes 10 minutes

1 large ripe mango
grated zest and juice of ½ lime
2 kiwi fruit, peeled
2 passion fruits
400 g 0% fat natural Greek yogurt
8 mini meringues

Ready-made meringues add both crunch and sweetness to this easily assembled dessert, while the tropical fruit flavours offset the sweetness perfectly.

Peel the mango using a swivel-headed peeler, or use a serrated knife. Cut the flesh away from the central stone and chop it into chunky pieces. Place in a bowl with the lime zest and juice.

Slice the kiwis into half-moons and add to the mango. Cut the passion fruit in half and squeeze the seeds and pulp out. Mix all the fruit together.

Layer up the fruit and yogurt in 4 bowls or dessert glasses, crumbling in the meringues as you go.

Serve straightaway while the meringue pieces are still crunchy.

Variation

For a berry fruit crush, quarter 250 g strawberries and mix with 150 g raspberries and 75 g blueberries, plus a little grated orange zest. The **ProPoints** values per serving will be 2.

WHITE CHOCOLATE Puds
with *Raspberry* Sauce

4 *ProPoints values per serving*
ProPoints values per recipe 18

Serves 4

Takes 15 minutes + cooling + chilling

calorie controlled cooking spray
4 sheets leaf gelatine
300 ml skimmed milk
25 g caster sugar
40 g white chocolate, chopped
150 g fat-free natural yogurt
4 tablespoons Weight Watchers crème fraîche, or similar
½ teaspoon vanilla extract
250 g raspberries
1 tablespoon icing sugar

These cool, creamy set puds are served with a vibrant raspberry sauce and fresh berries and look really pretty.

Spray 4 mini pudding basins with the cooking spray. Submerge the leaf gelatine in a bowl of cold water and leave to soak for about 5 minutes.

Heat the milk and sugar in a pan until starting to bubble at the edges. Remove the pan from the heat.

Squeeze the excess water from the gelatine and add to the hot milk. Stir to dissolve, then stir in the white chocolate until it has melted. Cool the mixture to room temperature. This process can be speeded up by standing the pan in a larger bowl of cold water and stirring occasionally as the mixture cools.

In a mixing bowl, whisk together the yogurt, crème fraîche and vanilla extract, then blend in the white chocolate milk. Pour into the prepared pudding basins, cover with cling film and chill in the fridge for 2 hours or until set.

Make the sauce by blending 150 g of the raspberries with the icing sugar. Sieve the sauce to remove the seeds.

Turn the white chocolate puds out of their basins. Top with the remaining raspberries and drizzle with the raspberry sauce.

APPLE & *Ginger* Fool

 Serves 4
Takes 15 minutes + chilling

450 g cooking apples, peeled, cored
and chopped
40 g caster sugar
125 g pot low fat custard, chilled
(ensure gluten free)
150 g 0% fat natural Greek yogurt
3 pieces stem ginger in syrup,
drained

A fruity but creamy chilled dessert, enlivened with a spicy kick of stem ginger. Divine accompanied by a Ginger Oat Cookie (see page 198) for an additional 2 **ProPoints** values per serving, if you have **ProPoints** to spare.

Place the prepared apples in a lidded pan with the sugar and 3 tablespoons of water. Cover and cook for 8–10 minutes, or until the apple is soft and collapsing.

Blend the apples to a smooth purée in a food processor, or using a hand-held blender. Cool completely.

Whisk the custard and 100 g of the yogurt together until smooth and then fold in the apple purée.

Slice 1 piece of stem ginger into matchsticks for garnish, and chop the other 2 pieces into small dice. Stir the diced ginger into the apple fool mixture and divide between 4 glasses.

Spoon the rest of the yogurt on top of the fools and garnish them with the stem ginger matchsticks. Cover and chill for at least 1 hour before serving.

Layered CHEESECAKE Sundaes

6 *ProPoints* values per serving
ProPoints values per recipe 25

Serves 4
Takes 10 minutes + chilling

25 g dark chocolate
40 g digestive biscuits
15 g toasted chopped hazelnuts
300 g low fat soft cheese
125 g 0% fat natural Greek yogurt
25 g caster sugar
½ teaspoon vanilla extract

A tantalising combination of layers: crunchy, nutty crumbs and smooth, creamy cheesecake, set off by dark chocolate.

Finely grate about a quarter of the chocolate into a small bowl and reserve for the topping. Pop it in the fridge, covered, so that it doesn't get too warm and start to melt.

Blitz the rest of the chocolate and the digestive biscuits to crumbs in a food processor, then stir in the hazelnuts to make the chocolate crunch layer.

Tip the soft cheese into a bowl and beat in the yogurt, sugar and vanilla extract until smooth.

Layer up the chocolate crunch mixture and the cheesecake mixture alternately in 4 dessert glasses. Sprinkle the grated chocolate on top. Chill for 1–2 hours, or until ready to serve.

Variations

Go fruity: omit the dark chocolate from the recipe and replace with 150 g raspberries (fresh or defrosted), lightly crushed with 1 tablespoon icing sugar. Layer the crushed berries up with the hazelnut crumb mixture and the cheesecake mixture. The *ProPoints* values per serving will be 6.

GF If you swap the digestive biscuits for gluten free digestives you can enjoy this dessert the gluten free way.

Cook's tip If you don't have a food processor to prepare the crumb mixture, simply place the digestive biscuits in a plastic food bag and crush, using a rolling pin or the base of a heavy pan. Grate the chocolate and stir it into the crumbs with the hazelnuts.

Bubbly Jellies

 ProPoints values per serving
ProPoints values per recipe 1

 Serves 4
Takes 10 minutes + chilling

 1 sachet sugar-free lemon and lime
    jelly (ensure gluten free)
250 ml boiling water
juice of 1 lemon
150 g raspberries
100 g blueberries
2 teaspoons chopped fresh mint
300 ml diet lemonade

A lovely summery dessert — you can actually feel the fizzy bubbles in the jelly.

Tip the contents of the jelly sachet into a large bowl. Pour in the boiling water and stir well to dissolve. Add the lemon juice, cool and then chill in the fridge for 1 hour, or until the jelly is almost ready to set (it will start to look thicker).

Gently mix the raspberries, blueberries and mint together and divide between 4 glasses or bowls.

Slowly mix the lemonade into the almost-set jelly then pour it over the berries in the glasses. Cover with cling film and chill in the fridge for 2 hours, or until set.

> *Cook's tip* Chilling the jelly to near setting-point before adding the lemonade means that you trap more of the lemonade bubbles as the jelly sets. However, if you don't have time to do this, simply add the lemonade to the dissolved jelly crystals and use straightaway. You'll still get a lightly sparkling jelly – just not quite as bubbly and fizzy.

Strawberry Layered Puds

M Serves 4
Preparation time 10 minutes
V Cooking time 30 minutes + cooling

400 g strawberries, halved or
    quartered depending on size
1 tablespoon balsamic vinegar
6 teaspoons clear honey
60 g porridge oats
300 g 0% fat natural Greek yogurt
salt and freshly ground black
    pepper

Roasting strawberries gives them an intense, jammy flavour. It might sound rather odd to season them with salt and pepper, but adding a tiny amount of savoury seasoning really helps to bring out the fruitiness. Utterly delicious!

Preheat the oven to Gas Mark 4/180°C/fan oven 160°C.

Place the prepared strawberries in a single layer in a shallow baking dish. Season very lightly and drizzle with the balsamic vinegar and 4 teaspoons of the honey. Stir to combine. Roast in the oven for 30 minutes, stirring halfway through, until the strawberries are darker in colour, smell jammy and are surrounded by syrupy juices. Leave to cool.

Meanwhile, mix together the rest of the honey and the oats. Spread out in a shallow layer on a baking tray. Toast in the oven for 8–10 minutes until golden and crisp. Set aside to cool.

To assemble, sprinkle a layer of honeyed oats in the bottom of 4 dessert glasses or bowls. Add the yogurt and then spoon the strawberry compote on top. Finish off with another layer of the crunchy oats and serve.

> *Cook's tip* The strawberry compote is a great way to use slightly over-ripe strawberries, especially if they are being sold off cheaply.

APRICOT & Raspberry
Popovers

 Serves 6
Preparation time 10 minutes
Cooking time 25 minutes

411 g can apricot halves in juice, drained

75 g plain flour

a pinch of salt

25 g caster sugar

2 eggs

½ teaspoon vanilla extract

175 ml skimmed milk

calorie controlled cooking spray

150 g raspberries

500 g carton low fat custard, to serve

½ teaspoon icing sugar, to dust

These delectable popovers are rather like a sweet version of toad-in-the-hole!

Preheat the oven to Gas Mark 6/200°C/fan oven 180°C. Place a 12-hole non-stick muffin tin or bun tin in the oven to preheat for 5 minutes.

Cut the apricot halves in two and pat dry on absorbent kitchen paper.

Sift the flour into a mixing bowl with the salt, then stir in the sugar. Make a well in the centre and break in the eggs. Add the vanilla extract and gradually whisk together, adding the milk as you go.

Spray the hot muffin or bun tin with the cooking spray. Pour in the batter to make 12 popovers. Drop the apricot pieces and raspberries into the batter then bake on the centre shelf for 20–25 minutes until the popovers are puffed up, golden brown and set.

Meanwhile, heat the custard. Remove the hot popovers from the tin and dust with icing sugar.

Serve 2 popovers per person, with warm custard poured over the top.

Pineapple
Tatins

 6 *ProPoints* values per serving
ProPoints values per recipe 26

 Serves 4
Preparation time 15 minutes

 Cooking time 15 minutes

425 g can pineapple slices in juice
1 tablespoon low fat spread
1 tablespoon caster sugar
a pinch of ground cinnamon
200 g puff pastry

A tropical twist on the traditional French dessert made with apples. Serve with a scoop of low fat ice cream for an additional 2 *ProPoints* values per serving.

Preheat the oven to Gas Mark 6/200°C/fan oven 180°C.

Drain the pineapple slices, reserving the juice. Pat the pineapple dry on absorbent kitchen paper.

Melt the low fat spread in a non-stick frying pan and sprinkle in the sugar. Add the pineapple slices and cook on a high heat for 2½ minutes each side until caramelised.

Sprinkle in the cinnamon and add 6 tablespoons of the reserved pineapple juice to the pan. Let the sauce bubble for 1 minute then remove from the heat.

Stack 2 caramelised pineapple rings in each compartment of a 4-hole Yorkshire pudding tin, and spoon in the sauce.

Roll out the pastry to a 25 cm square and cut out 4 x 12 cm discs (use an upturned saucer or bowl as a guide). Press on top of the pineapple in the tin, tucking in the edges of the pastry. Bake in the oven for 15 minutes until the pastry is puffed up and golden brown.

Place a clean chopping board on top of the tray and quickly flip over to remove the pineapple tatins. Serve immediately.

Swedish APPLE & ALMOND Bake

 ProPoints values per serving
ProPoints values per recipe 31

 Serves 6
Preparation time 15 minutes
Cooking time 30 minutes + resting

8 eating apples, peeled, cored and
    sliced
½ teaspoon ground cinnamon
grated zest and juice of ½ lemon
90 g caster sugar
125 g self-raising flour, sifted
a pinch of salt
125 g fat-free natural yogurt
55 g low fat spread, melted
15 g flaked almonds
½ teaspoon icing sugar, to dust

Based on a Scandinavian pudding, the lemon and cinnamon-scented apples, with their light spongy topping, will smell lush as they bake.

Preheat the oven to Gas Mark 4/180°C/fan oven 160°C.

Place the sliced apples in a 23 cm diameter baking dish with the cinnamon, lemon zest and juice. Toss to combine.

Mix the sugar and flour together with the salt in a mixing bowl then stir in the yogurt and melted low fat spread.

Dollop the batter on top of the apples to cover, then sprinkle with the almonds. Bake on the centre shelf for 30 minutes.

Leave to stand for 10 minutes, and dust with the icing sugar to serve.

MARBLED *Chocolate* Risotto

ProPoints **values per serving**
ProPoints **values per recipe 25**

GF

HC

V

Serves 4
Preparation time 5 minutes
Cooking time 40 minutes + resting

2 teaspoons low fat spread
110 g arborio rice
10 g cocoa powder
40 g caster sugar
600 ml skimmed milk
½ teaspoon vanilla extract
20 g white chocolate drops

A cross between a traditional rice pudding and risotto, flavoured with everyone's favourite ingredient – chocolate.

Preheat the oven to Gas Mark 2/150°C/fan oven 130°C.

Melt the low fat spread in a lidded ovenproof casserole. Add the arborio rice and cook, stirring for 1 minute. Add the cocoa powder and sugar, quickly followed by the milk.

Bring the mixture almost to the boil, stirring occasionally so that the rice doesn't form clumps. Cover the casserole with a lid and place in the oven.

Cook for 35–40 minutes, stirring occasionally, until the rice is tender and has absorbed most of the liquid.

Remove from the oven and stir in the vanilla extract. Scatter the white chocolate drops on top of the risotto and replace the lid. Leave to stand for 5 minutes.

As you spoon out the dessert, the white chocolate will marble through the chocolate risotto. Serve straightaway.

INDEX

About the author

TAMSIN BURNETT-HALL has written seven cookbooks for Weight Watchers, including *The Complete Kitchen*. After training at the prestigious Leiths School of Food and Wine, she started her career working as a cookery assistant to Delia Smith, with whom she worked for eight years on a variety of projects including filming TV series, working on books, preparing food for photography and magazine publishing. In her freelance writing career Tamsin has worked for a wide variety of food magazines, but always relishes the challenge of coming up with inspiring new healthy and delicious *ProPoints* value friendly recipes.